If We Are Saved, Are We Promised Heaven?

BRANDON DOVER

ISBN 979-8-89243-233-7 (paperback)
ISBN 979-8-89243-234-4 (digital)

Copyright © 2024 by Brandon Dover

All rights reserved. No part of this publication may be reproduced, distributed, or transmitted in any form or by any means, including photocopying, recording, or other electronic or mechanical methods without the prior written permission of the publisher. For permission requests, solicit the publisher via the address below.

Christian Faith Publishing
832 Park Avenue
Meadville, PA 16335
www.christianfaithpublishing.com

Unless otherwise noted, all scripture references are from New King James Version (NKJV).

All the Greek references are from the Greek Interlinear/Concordance and Thayers Greek Lexicon found in the Blue Letter Bible app.

Printed in the United States of America

May all glory and praise be to the Almighty God,
our Father in heaven above, and to my Lord
and Savior, Jesus the Christ Almighty.

Contents

The Beginning vi

1 Giving Your Heart to God 1

    Surrender to Him 2
    Allow Him to Lead You 4
    Love Him 6
    Guard Your Heart 7
    Free Will 9
    Resist Temptation 10
    His Protection 12
    Being Tested 15
    Accepting His Love 16

2 Learning the Gospel 19

    Escape Vengeance 20
    The Word 23
    Receiving His Testimony 30
    Learn from Him 32
    Bread of Life 34
    Abide in Him 37
    Knowing God 38
    Spirit and Truth 42
    Living for Christ 43
    Denying Oneself 46
    He Promises 48

3 Becoming a New Creation..51

   Born Again..52
   Water and Spirit...54
   Receiving His Spirit..56
   Baptized in Christ..57
   The Spirit..66
   Our Commitment..67

4 Becoming Sons of God..69

   Faith in Christ...70
   The Adoption 74
   The Anointing 79
   Fruit of the Spirit 85

5 Salvation and Heaven...91

   A Free Ride from Christ..92
   The Sugarcoated Version 95
   Salvation 100
   Believing in Christ 103
   Christ as Our Lord..105
   Heaven and the Way 108

6 Entering Heaven 111

   Gathering or Scattering 113
   Conscious Effort 114
   The Narrow Gate 115
   Referring to Believers 118
   Being Cast Out 122
   Hot or Cold 138

The End...141

The Beginning

"I am the Alpha and the Omega, the Beginning and the End," Says the Lord, "Who is and who was and who is to come, the Almighty."

—Revelation 1:8

Lately I have found myself caught up in the discussion about if we are saved, are we promised we are going to heaven? Many say we are. Just about every church and pastor preach this all the time. They tell us that "if we confess with our mouth the Lord Jesus and believe in our heart that God has raised Him from the dead, you will be saved" (Rom. 10:9). And this is true. It's what the Bible tells us, so it must be true. And as you pray this confession, you ask God to forgive you of your sins and the Christ Jesus to come into your heart to be your Lord and Savior. Then when you're finished saying this prayer, they say you're saved and going to heaven. Praise God salvation can come so easily through His grace. But does God say that once we make this confession, we are guaranteed to go to heaven? Jesus tells us we are saved, but does salvation guarantee the kingdom of heaven?

The answer to this question is not for me to give; only God has that answer. We can find that answer by analyzing and searching the scriptures in the Bible to see what God tells us. That is what I encourage you to do as I attempt to do the same. As we go through the scriptures and take a closer look at God's Word, you will be awfully surprised in what the Lord Jesus says about going to heaven and how to get there.

IF WE ARE SAVED, ARE WE PROMISED HEAVEN?

It is going to be real shock to you when you find out what it actually takes to achieve the ultimate goal of going to heaven and that most of everything you've been taught in church about heaven has been a deception or a sugarcoated version of the truth. I'm sure there are many of you who are ready to defend everything you have been taught. Please understand I am not here to attack or discredit what you believe. I only wish to bring to light what the Word of God tells us by inspiring you to search the scriptures.

There are many scriptures in the Bible that the churches don't elaborate on; they gloss right over them. They don't want to preach on them because they are afraid they may offend their congregation and the seats won't remain full. So they give a sugarcoated version of the gospel to make people feel good, thinking they can win souls for Christ. But are they really winning souls for Christ if they aren't preaching the whole truth?

Why are so many "Christians" living in poverty, broken, and in misery? God says, "You shall lend to many and you shall not borrow" (Deut. 28:12), "You will be the head and not the tail; you shall be above only, and not beneath" (Deut. 28:13), "That your joy may be full" (John 15:11). Why isn't the body of Christ, those who call themselves "Christians," experiencing God's promises?

Why do you think so many "Christians" are called hypocrites, more so today than ever before? Or here's an even better question to ask yourself, "Why are we not seeing the miracles, healings, and power demonstrated by the first-century church in the book of Acts in our churches today?" God hasn't changed; it's the same gospel and the same Holy Spirit. The only thing that has changed is what is preached and believed!

When you finish this book, you will have the answers.

1

Giving Your Heart to God

> That which was from the beginning, which we have seen with our eyes, which we have looked upon, and our hands have handled, concerning the Word of life—the life was manifested, and we have seen, and bear witness, and declare to you that eternal life which was with the Father and was manifested to us—that which we have seen and heard we declare to you, that you also may have fellowship with us; and truly our fellowship is with the Father and His Son Jesus Christ. And these things we write to you that your joy may be full.
>
> —1 John 1:1–4

In the gospel according to Matthew, there is recorded one of the greatest sermons of all time, the Sermon on the Mount. In this sermon, Jesus gives us a detailed description of the characteristics that a Christian is to possess. In the beginning of this sermon, Jesus states, blessed are those who possess certain characteristics. Many call these the Beatitudes, which originates from the word "beati" (meaning "blessed"). There are nine Beatitudes in number, but only seven refer to character.

One of these characteristics is a pure heart. Jesus states,

> Blessed are the pure in heart, for they shall see God. (Matt. 5:8)

Being pure in heart is being free from all evil desires and purposes, having the heart to live a life comparable to that of a divine nature, the very divine nature in which we were created from. John tells us,

> Beloved, now we are children of God; and it has not yet been revealed what we shall be, but we know that when He is revealed, we shall be like Him, for we shall see Him as He is. And everyone who has this hope in Him purifies himself, just as He is pure. (1 John 3:2–3)

Peter tells us,

> Therefore gird up the loins of your mind, be sober, and rest your hope fully upon the grace that is to be brought to you at the revelation of Jesus Christ; as obedient children, not conforming yourselves to the former lusts, as in your ignorance; but as He who called you is holy, you also be holy in all your conduct, because it is written, "Be holy, for I am holy." (1 Pet. 1:13–16)

You must purify yourself and your heart and become holy as He is holy; and by doing this, you shall see God, now and in the life to come.

Surrender to Him

So how do we go about making ourselves pure, or how do we purify our heart so that we may see God? I believe the first step in doing this is by surrendering our heart fully to Him. This is a very difficult thing for many to do, especially the older one gets. What happens is the longer we live in the world, the more attached to it we become. The more time we spend going to school and pursuing our careers, developing relationships, and having children, the closer and more attached we become to these things. The more time we spend with or doing something, the more we come to love it. This is the very reason that it is difficult to forsake our lives and surrender our hearts to God and the Lord Jesus.

Turning your life over to the Lord Jesus and God can seem overbearing to some, especially when they have lived a very ungodly life. Shame and resentment, or remorse and even fear can leave a person with the feeling of being unworthy to come to God. I hear it said quite often, "As soon as I get right and change my ways, I will go to church and seek God" or "They wouldn't allow a person like me in church" or "I've done too many bad things in my life for God to ever forgive me, much less ever love me. So why waste my time?" Many people allow their feelings of unworthiness from the things they do prevent them from coming to the Lord. When the truth is, it's because of these very things we do wrong that we need to come to the Lord so that He can heal us. And these are the same thoughts and feelings that God allows us to experience, in order to make us realize just how much we need Him to fix and heal us.

> Return, backsliding children, says the Lord; I will not cause My anger to fall on you. For I am merciful, says the Lord; I will not remain angry forever. Only acknowledge your iniquity, that you have transgressed against the Lord your God, and have scattered your charms to alien deities under every green tree, and you have not obeyed My voice, says the Lord. (Jer. 3:12–13)

You see, God just wants His backsliding children to come to Him.

In Jeremiah 3:13, God tells us to acknowledge the very things that we allow to prevent us from coming to Him. He says only acknowledge your iniquity, that you're not a good person; that you have transgressed against Him, doing things that aren't morally right and sinful in nature; that you have scattered your charms to alien deities, having idolized ungodly things (such as drugs, fornication, lewdness, pornography, gambling, money, etc.) or anything one may idolize more than God; and that you have not obeyed His commands. Are these not the very things we acknowledge we do and allow them to make us feel unworthy enough to come to God? When this is exactly what He wants us to do, realize and acknowledge that we do these things and are unworthy so He can be merciful and heal us.

> Return, O backsliding children, says the LORD; for I am married to you. I will take you, one from a city and two from a family, and I will bring you to Zion. (Jer. 3:14)

God says come to Him all you broken and backsliding people, for He loves us as a married couple and wants a relationship with you. He says He will bring those few who do come to Him to Zion, a place of peace and comfort. God loves you; He loves you like a bride and wants you to come to Him.

Allow Him to Lead You

No matter what you have done in your life, just acknowledge it and give your heart to Him. Then God says,

> And I will give you shepherds according to My heart, who will feed you with knowledge and understanding. (Jer. 3:15)

Acknowledge that you sin and give your heart to God and He will give you shepherds who will feed you with knowledge and understanding. It doesn't matter how bad you may think you are—God loves you and will send a shepherd to help you.

Jesus said,

> I am the good shepherd. The good shepherd gives His life for the sheep. (John 10:11)

And did not Jesus say,

> Take My yoke upon you and learn from Me. (Matt. 11:29)

And did not Jesus also say,

> If you love Me, keep My commandments. And I will pray the Father, and He will give you another Helper, that He may abide with you forever. (John 14:15–16)

Jesus also said,

> If you then, being evil, know how to give good gifts to your children, how much more will your heavenly Father give the Holy Spirit to those who ask Him! (Luke 11:13)

From out of His unyielding grace and never-ending mercy, from out of the love in His heart, God has sent us two shepherds who will feed us with knowledge and understanding. All we have to do is turn and open our hearts to Him, acknowledge our sin, and ask Him to come into our hearts; and He will give us shepherds who will help us.

Jesus said He is the good shepherd, that the good shepherd gives His life for His sheep. His sheep are those who follow Him. He leads them, guides them, feeds them, and teaches them. Those who follow Jesus spend time with Him, learn from Him, trust Him, and love

Him. When you give your heart to someone, you spend time with that person, learn about that person, and love that person.

Love Him

Jesus said, "He who does not love Me does not keep My words." Is He saying that if you don't keep His Word, then you really don't love Him? I believe that is what He said. So let's think about this for a moment: if you love someone or something, you spend time with whom or what you love. Love isn't automatic; it takes time and attention to develop. Again I say to you, it's after you have devoted your time and attention to something that you begin to love it.

For instance, let's consider the first time you met that special someone in your life. You may have thought you loved them at first sight, but I'm sure it was a mixture of emotions stemming from desire and attraction. And from that desire and attraction you wanted to spend every moment you could with that person—getting to know them better, finding their likes and dislikes, searching for the things you may have in common, things of that sort. You gave that person your attention and spent time developing a relationship. From your desire and attraction, you wanted to spend time and give your attention to that individual; and after a while, you grew to love that person.

Let me use another example, in case the person reading this never experienced the dating process. Some people love sports, but they weren't born loving sports. Believe it or not, for those sports lovers, it's true. You weren't born loving sports. Anyway, it wasn't until that person was attracted to the sport and actually tried it or watched it that they began to desire the sport. The more time they put into the sport, the more they started to really enjoy it. Then once they gave a considerable amount of their time and attention to the sport, they began to love it.

So you see, it takes your time and attention to begin to love someone or something. It's the same with God—if you truly love God, you will give Him your attention and spend time with Him.

You will take time getting to know Him; you will give Him your attention to develop a relationship with Him. How do you get to know God? It is by spending time reading His Word and giving Him your attention in prayer; this is how you get to know God. You develop a relationship with Him through His Word. And as that relationship develops, you begin to love Him and trust Him. When you love Him, He comes and makes His home with you. He gives you His Spirit; He fills your heart with true love.

Guard Your Heart

Now let's get back to our heart and why it is so important to God. Why do you think God wants our heart to be pure? And why is God so interested in our heart to begin with? Well, throughout the Bible, God tells us about the heart continuously. In Proverbs it says,

> Keep your heart with all diligence, for out of it
> spring the issues of life. (Prov. 4:23)

The heart is the very essence of your soul. And God, who gave us these souls, gave us a strict charge over them, to guard them and protect them. We are to guard our heart or keep our heart with all diligence. We are to treat it as the most important thing in our life and protect it with all we have. For out of it spring the issues of life; from out of our heart is whom we are.

The direction in which we set our heart determines the outcome of our lives. King Solomon wrestled with this very issue when he fell from his reign. Solomon is said to be the wisest man in history, but he allowed his heart to be drawn away from God by the pleasures of this world. Solomon tells us,

> And I set my heart to seek and search out by wisdom concerning all that is done under heaven; this burdensome task God has given to the sons

of man, by which they may be exercised. (Eccles. 1:13)

You are given the task of guiding your heart; you are to guard over it, watch what is planted in it, so that you may guide it and lead it in a direction that will keep you safe and prosper you.

In this day and age, it is difficult to guard our hearts especially with everything that is in the news media, on television, in the movies, all over the radio, on the Internet, and even in the gaming technology. The majority of it all is negative-thought input, filled with immoral behavior, sex, anger, death, and destruction. Even the cartoons our children watch are now filled with adult content. Everything we listen to and watch is being planted into our hearts; it's being seeded into our subconscious thinking. A major part of what we call entertainment is actually making us worse than we already are.

Jesus said,

> What comes out of a man, that defiles a man. For from within, out of the heart of men, proceed evil thoughts, adulteries, fornications, murders, thefts, covetousness, wickedness, deceit, lewdness, an evil eye, blasphemy, pride, foolishness. All these evil things come from within and defile a man. (Mark 7:20–23)

Jesus tells us that these are the very things that defile us. So if these are the things that we are watching on TV or in the movies, and these are the things we are listening about on the radio, and these are the things we are flooding our hearts with, how do you think we are going to act? These are the very things we should be guarding our hearts from. And we wonder why the world is so messed up. It's because the world, for the most part, doesn't know God and guard its hearts.

The heart of mankind is the focus of God; it is the very thing He desires.

> Would not God search this out? For He knows
> the secrets of the heart. (Ps. 44:21)

God knows our heart, and He knows that our heart is who we are, and who we are for, it's our desires, our dislikes; it's the very essence of our souls, and it drives us to do the things we do, developing the kind of character that we are as a person. And God wants our hearts to be for Him and pure like Him.

Free Will

You've heard that the devil is out to get your soul or the devil wants to steal your soul. Or maybe you've heard the saying "He sold his soul to the devil"? There were all kinds of movies and songs made on this very topic. That's because it's true, the devil is out to gain souls. The devil knows, just like God, that the souls of mankind are the heart. And the devil, just like God, knows that whatever mankind decides to set his heart on or give his heart to, it's that very thing man will follow.

God gave man charge over his own heart, and with that came the freedom to choose what he wants to do with his heart. This freedom is what we call free will, the freedom to will our heart to whatever we choose. God allowed mankind the freedom to follow whatever our hearts desire. God did this for a very specific reason.

This is the reason for free will; we have the freedom to choose God or deny God. And without free will, there could be no true love. You see, our free will isn't about having the freedom to choose what we are going to wear or what kind of car we drive; it's about choosing whom we are going to live our life for. Are we going to live our life for God, or are we going to live our life for ourselves? Do we choose God, or do we choose this world? Do we choose this world and all its alluring things and pleasures, this so-called physical reality in which we think we need to survive? Or do we choose an Almighty God of whom we cannot touch or see, an all-powerful Spirit that we must have faith in and believe in?

This is a very difficult task for many, but this very task is what shows true love. If we were created without having this choice, this free will, and we were created to only know God and nothing else, to love Him only, then it wouldn't really be love. We would be like robots programmed only to know one thing, and that would be forced love. True love can only exist when there is a choice to love one thing over another.

So you see, God gave us this freedom to choose what we want to set our hearts on, to see if we truly love and worship Him in heart and spirit. Then to test the purity of this love, God allowed an adversary to come into play to tempt mankind to follow his own desires rather than God's desires. Because God wants true worshippers to follow Him, He wants those who truly love Him. God created you and gave you life, and now He wants to know what you're going to put first in the life He gave you.

Resist Temptation

We see the devil, or Satan, as this evil thing out to destroy us; and this may be true. Then one may ask, "If God created everything, in which He did, then why create something so bad? But is Satan really bad, or does he have a job to do?" If you read in the scriptures, in the book of Job, you will see that Satan attends the team meetings and answers to God.

> Now there was a day when the sons of God came to present themselves before the LORD, and Satan also came among them. And the LORD said to Satan, "From where do you come?" So Satan answered the LORD and said, "From going to and fro on the earth, and from walking back and forth on it." Then the LORD said to Satan, "Have you considered My servant Job, that there is none like him on the earth, a blameless and upright man, one who fears God and shuns evil?" (Job 1:6–8)

> Again there was a day when the sons of God came to present themselves before the Lord, and Satan came also among them to present himself before the Lord. And the Lord said to Satan, "From where do you come?" So Satan answered the Lord and said, "From going to and fro on the earth, and from walking back and forth on it." Then the Lord said to Satan, "Have you considered My servant Job, that there is none like him on the earth, a blameless and upright man, one who fears God and shuns evil? And still he holds fast to his integrity, although you incited Me against him, to destroy him without cause." (Job 2:1–3)

We read here that God has meetings with the angels and Satan is there among them, but why? If Satan is God's enemy, then what is he doing at the team meetings with God and His angels? And why is God conversing with Satan about His servant Job? Is it because Satan is an angel too? All God's angels are held accountable for the jobs they are assigned to do. And could it be that even the fallen angels are held accountable too? Satan is often called the accuser or the tempter. Could that be his job, to accuse and tempt?

> Thus says the Lord God, "You were the seal of perfection, full of wisdom and perfect in beauty. You were in Eden, the garden of God; every precious stone was your covering: the sardis, topaz, and diamond, beryl, onyx, and jasper, sapphire, turquoise, and emerald with gold. The workmanship of your timbrels and pipes was prepared for you on the day you were created. You were the anointed cherub who covers; I established you; you were on the holy mountain of God; you walked back and forth in the midst of fiery stones. You were perfect in your ways from the

> day you were created, till iniquity was found in you." (Ezek. 28:12–15)

Could it be that God created an angel so beautiful, so intelligent, so powerful, and gave him so much authority that it would affect his ego and pride, allowing this angel's pride to tempt him to go against God and want to be like Him, so much so that it would cause this angel to become His adversary to fulfill a purpose, creating a plan with the purpose to test the hearts of mankind? Just a thought to ponder on, especially when you look at the whole scheme of creation entirely.

If you read the book of Job, you will see that it is about Job's heart, whether it was for God or for himself. And Satan's job was to tempt Job into cursing God or to deny God for his life and this world. Satan's job was to tempt the heart of Job, pure and simple. Satan used every means possible to draw Job away from holding fast to trusting in God. Satan killed and destroyed all that Job had, even ravaged him with sickness and disease. Satan used Job's wife and his friends; he used every worldly thing he could think of to pull Job's heart from God. And Satan does the same with us; that is his job. Satan's job is to tempt our hearts from God, and he is good at it. Could this be how God finds those whose heart is truly for Him, those who truly love Him?

His Protection

Now don't be discouraged and think that God is out to harm you by using Satan; that is not so. God says,

> For I know the thoughts that I think towards you, says the Lord, thoughts of peace and not of evil, to give you a future and a hope. (Jer. 29:11)

This is true, because we can look back and see what God did for Job before Satan tempted him, how God protected him. Satan said to God,

> Have You not made a hedge around him, around his household, and around all that he has on every side? You have blessed the work of his hands, and his possessions have increased in the land. (Job 1:10)

Why did God protect Job? Was it because his heart was for God?

> There was a man in the land of Uz, whose name was Job; and that man was blameless and upright, and one who feared God and shunned evil. (Job 1:1)

Job's heart was for God, and it shunned evil. He followed God's commands and was obedient and blameless. Job was upright and just. His heart was pure. Therefore, he had God's protection.

We gain God's protection by having a heart for God and not for evil.

> If you diligently obey the voice of the Lord your God, to observe carefully all His commandments, that the Lord your God will set you high above all nations of the earth. And all these blessings shall come upon you and overtake you, because you obey the voice of the Lord your God. (Deut. 28:1–2)

God wants to put us high above everyone else and overtake us with blessings. These blessings He wants to pour upon us will protect us and keep us safe from sickness, poverty, and our enemies.

> Blessed shall be the fruit of your body. (Deut. 28:4)
>
> The Lord will cause your enemies who rise against you to be defeated before your face; they shall come out against you one way and flee before you seven ways. (Deut. 28:7)
>
> The Lord will command the blessing on you in your storehouses and in all to which you set your hand. (Deut. 28:8)

God wants to protect us from our enemies, keep us healthy, and prosper us by blessing everything we do.

The scriptures tell us,

> My son, give attention to my words; incline your ears to my sayings. Do not let them depart from your eyes; keep them in the midst of your heart; for they are life to those who find them, and health to all their flesh. (Prov. 4:20–22)

Here again, we see that if we keep the words of God in our heart, they will give us life and keep us healthy; they protect us.

Then God says,

> Then you will call upon Me and go and pray to Me, and I will listen to you. And you will seek Me and find Me, when you search for Me with all your heart. (Jer. 29:12–13)

When our heart is for God, He protects us and listens to us, and we shall see Him. This is why it is so important for us to give our heart to God, in order to gain His Spirit and protection, so He can give us peace and prosper us.

Being Tested

Don't think God won't allow us to be tested, because He will. Let's go all the way back to the beginning, back when Adam and Eve were in the garden of Eden. Was God not allowing Adam's and Eve's hearts to be tested when they were being tempted by the devil? Do you think God didn't know what was going on when the serpent was tempting Eve to eat of the tree of the knowledge of good and evil?

If we are to believe that God is omniscient, all-knowing, that He knows and sees everything all the time, then we are to believe that He knew what was happening then too. I mean, do you think God was just taking a little nap at that moment and missed the whole scene between the serpent and Eve, and Eve giving some of the fruit to Adam? Of course not. He was watching it all the whole time. He was watching to see if their hearts were for Him or for themselves and this world.

Let's go back even further, before the serpent tempted Adam and Eve, to the first command God gave man.

> And the LORD God commanded the man, saying, "Of every tree of the garden you may freely eat; but of the tree of the knowledge of good and evil you shall not eat, for in the day that you eat of it you shall surely die." (Gen. 2:16–17)

Why put the tree in the garden in the first place? Why would God put something that could kill Adam in his midst? Could the tree have been a test to see if Adam loved God and would be obedient to His command? You see, God gave mankind the free will to choose, and Adam had the choice to choose what God desired or what he desired.

It wasn't God's desire for Adam to die; he was meant to live forever. That is why God commanded Adam not to eat from the tree; He knew it would harm him. God gave Adam a command that would protect him because God loved Adam. God gave Adam the freedom to follow Him and live forever; all he had to do is follow

God's one command. It was the first test of man's heart, to see if man would truly follow God.

God's plan for Adam was to have peace and not evil; it was to prosper him and give him a future. But Adam didn't choose God's plan; he chose his own desire instead. He chose to follow his woman, being the world; he chose his flesh, eating of the food; he chose his ego, something that would make him wise. Adam chose to please himself other than God; his heart was for himself and not for God. He didn't listen to what God told him, the very thing that would give him peace and a future. So you see, from the very beginning, man didn't want to listen to what God told him; and it cost him pain and heartache.

Accepting His Love

Obviously, in the days of the Old Testament, the people weren't listening to what God was trying to tell them either. He sent them prophets telling the people to turn their hearts to God so He can protect them and give them peace and prosper them as well. But they didn't want to hear it; they loved the world and themselves more than they loved God, much like it is today.

God had to find another way to touch the hearts of mankind; so He sent His Son, Jesus the Christ, into the world. He sent Jesus to do what man couldn't do: to give His heart to God. So that mankind can have reconciliation with God through His Son, Jesus the Christ. We couldn't save ourselves, so He sent His Son to save us. What a loving God.

> For God so loved the world that He gave His only begotten Son, that whoever believes in Him should not perish but have everlasting life. For God did not send His Son into the world to condemn the world, but that the world through Him might be saved. (John 3:16–17)

God sent His Son into the world to touch the hearts of mankind so they may have reconciliation with Him, to change their hearts back to Him so that He may protect them and save them. God said,

> I will give you a new heart and put a new spirit within you; I will take the heart of stone out of your flesh and give you a heart of flesh. (Ezek. 36:26)

God sent His Son to change our hearts for Him so He can give us a new Spirit and save us.

Jesus said it very clearly,

> For the hearts of this people have grown dull. Their ears are hard of hearing, And their eyes they have closed, Lest they should see with their eyes and hear with their ears, Lest they should understand with their hearts and turn, So that I should heal them. (Matt. 13:15)

Our hearts have grown dull, or in other words, they are dying. And unless we look to Jesus and listen to what He tells us, perceive what He is saying, and turn our hearts to Him, He can't heal us. If we don't allow Jesus to heal our hearts, how can He save them? How can He give us His Spirit?

> Nor do they put new wine into old wineskins, or else the wineskins break, the wine is spilled, and the wineskins are ruined. But they put new wine into new wineskins, and both are preserved. (Matt. 9:17)

Is Jesus telling us here that He can't put a new Spirit into an old heart or a dead heart, but first the heart must be healed or made new before He can give it a new Spirit? Could Jesus be telling us that we need a new heart, a heart for God, in order to receive His

Spirit? Many say that He heals our heart and changes it with His Holy Spirit, that He gives us His Spirit first, and that is what changes us. This may be very well so, but either way we must surrender and give our heart to God so He can save us.

2

Learning the Gospel

> "All flesh is as grass, and all the glory of
> man as the flower of the grass.
> The grass withers, and its flower falls away, but
> the word of the Lord endures forever."
> Now this is the word which by the gospel was preached to you.
>
> —1 Peter 1:24–25

Some of you may be willing to give your heart to God and want to learn more about Him and the Christ Jesus but find the Bible to be difficult to read. Many look at the Bible the same as any other book and attempt to read it as they would a novel. They pick it up, open it to page 1, and start reading. Then when they get to about the fourth chapter and start seeing some of the Arabic names, names they can't even begin to pronounce, they give up. They put the Bible down, and some never pick it up again, which is quite understandable, meaning who would want to read something they can't understand?

This is why it is important for a person to know that the Bible isn't like any other book. It is very different and must be read differently. The Bible has sixty-six books, written over a period of approximately two thousand years, in three different languages, by forty different authors from three different continents. Its contents unerringly point to Christ, written by godly men, inspired and led by the Holy Spirit of God.

> And so we have the prophetic word confirmed, which you do well to heed as a light that shines in a dark place, until the day dawns and the morning star rises in your hearts; knowing this first, that no prophecy of Scripture is of any private interpretation, for prophecy never came by the will of man, but holy men of God spoke as they were moved by the Holy Spirit. (2 Pet. 1:19–21)

Escape Vengeance

I want to begin this chapter by first explaining the importance of why we must learn the gospel of Christ Jesus and the Word of God. In the second letter Paul wrote to the Thessalonians, he opens this letter by exhorting the brethren for their growing faith and love for one another. Then he goes on to say,

> Since it is a righteous thing with God to repay with tribulation those who trouble you, and to give you who are troubled rest with us when the Lord Jesus is revealed from heaven with His mighty angels, in flaming fire taking vengeance on those who do not know God, and on those who do not obey the gospel of our Lord Jesus Christ. (2 Thess. 1:7–8)

It is interesting that he mentions that God will take vengeance on those who do not know Him and on those who do not obey the gospel of our Lord Jesus Christ. Then Paul goes on to say,

> These shall be punished with everlasting destruction from the presence of the Lord and from the glory of His power, when He comes, in that Day, to be glorified in His saints and to be admired among all those who believe, because our testimony among you was believed. (2 Thess. 1:9–10)

There are a couple of key points Paul makes here in verses 9 and 10. One is punished with everlasting destruction from the presence of the Lord. Take note here, Paul mentions "from the presence of the Lord." Paul is making a point about separation, being separated from the presence of God. He also said they would be punished with everlasting destruction; he didn't say cast into the lake of fire or Hades. Also keep in mind that Paul was writing this letter to the church, speaking of those who do not obey the gospel or retain God in their knowledge. This is an issue I will come back to later in this book, because Jesus talks of this very issue many times throughout His ministry.

Second is in verse 10, he mentions those who believe, those who believe the testimony of the saints. The gospels are composed of the testimonies of the saints, inspired by the Holy Spirit, about the ministry and teachings of the Lord Jesus the Christ. It's through these testimonies that we learn the gospel of the Lord Jesus the Christ, and we must believe in them in order to believe in Christ Jesus. Believing is a key point throughout the gospel. Actually belief is a major factor in our salvation. As it says,

> One must confess the Lord Jesus and believe in their heart that God raised Jesus from the dead. (Rom. 10:9)

You must believe, just as Jesus mentions many times in His ministry, "He who believes in Me" (John 6:35, 6:47, 7:38, 11:25, 12:44, 14:12).

Since Paul tells us that the Lord will take vengeance on those who do not obey the gospel of our Lord Jesus the Christ, let us now search the gospels and see what the Lord Jesus tells us, especially since the words that Jesus spoke carry so much more power than any other. And I say power here because the Word of God is powerful, sharp enough to divide the soul from the spirit.

> For the word of God is living and powerful, and sharper than any two-edged sword, piercing even to the division of soul and spirit, and of joints and marrow, and is a discerner of the thoughts and intents of the heart. (Heb. 4:12)

The Word of God is so powerful it takes root in your heart, in your soul, in your spirit, in the bones and tissue of your body; it takes root and changes the way you think, your intents, how you feel, and how you act.

I believe, for someone to obey the gospel of our Lord Jesus, they must first understand it. And the only way to understand something is to spend time learning about it. In order to know and understand the gospel, you're going to have to read it. And to be quite honest with you, you're going to have to read it several times. You're going to have to study it and let it take root in your heart. And when you read the gospel, pray for understanding and wisdom concerning it because if you don't, you won't know God, you won't know the Lord Jesus the Christ, you won't know His gospel; and if you don't know the gospel, you can't obey it. And this, my friend, could very well determine your final destiny.

The Word

Let's take some time here and define the meaning of the "Word" of God so we can gain a better understanding of it and why it is so powerful and alive. The two major words in Greek used for the "Word of God" are *Logos* (masculine noun) and *Rhema* (neuter noun).

Logos. John states,

> In the beginning was the Word, and the Word was with God, and the Word was God. (John 1:1)

The "Word" here in Greek is *Logos* (log'-os), meaning

1. Of speech;
   a) A word, uttered by a living voice, embodies a conception or idea
   b) What someone has said
      1) A word
      2) The sayings of God
      3) Decree, mandate or order
      4) Of the moral precepts given by God
      5) Old Testament prophecy given by the prophets
      6) What is declared, a thought, declaration, aphorism, a weighty saying, a dictum, a maxim
   c) Discourse
      1) The act of speaking, speech
      2) The faculty of speech, skill and practice in speaking
      3) A kind or style of speaking
      4) A continuous speaking discourse – instruction

d) Doctrine, teaching
   e) Anything reported in speech; a narration, narrative
   f) Matter under discussion, thing spoken of, affair, a matter in dispute, case, suit at law
   g) The thing spoken of or talked about; event, deed
2. Its use as respect to the MIND alone
   a) Reason, the mental faculty of thinking, meditating, reasoning, calculating
   b) Account, i.e. regard, consideration
   c) Account, i.e. reckoning, score
   d) Account, i.e. answer or explanation in reference to judgment
   e) Relation, i.e. with whom as judge we stand in relation
      1) Reason would
   f) Reason, cause, ground
3. In John, denotes the essential Word of God, Jesus Christ, the personal wisdom and power in union with God, his minister in creation and government of the universe, the cause of all the world's life both physical and ethical, which for the procurement of man's salvation put on human nature in the person of Jesus the Messiah, the second person in the Godhead, and shone forth conspicuously from His words and deeds. (Strong's)

Note: A Greek philosopher named Heraclitus first used the term *Logos* around 600 BC to designate the divine reason or plan which coordinates a changing universe. This word was well suited to John's purpose in John 1. (Strong's)

As you can see here, the Word is a direct reference to the Lord Jesus the Christ and can be considered the very core of our nature—how we learn, what we say and how we speak, how our mind works, and the very things we think. God said,

> Let us make man in Our image, according to Our likeness. (Gen. 1:26)

> All things were made through Him, and without Him nothing was made that was made. In Him was life, and the life was the light of men. (John 1:3–4)

You see, we get the ability to think and communicate, the divine nature that makes us human beings, from the Word: Christ Jesus, God. Without Him, we have no life in us and are nothing.

John tells us,

> In the beginning was the Word, and the Word was with God, and the Word was God. (John 1:1)

And then,

> All things were made through Him [the Word], and without Him [the Word] nothing was made that was made. (John 1:3)

Ever since the beginning of creation, everything was created through the Word of God, and that Word was Jesus the Christ.

Now if you go back to the beginning of the Bible and you read the first chapter of Genesis, you will notice that when God spoke, things were made.

> Then God said, "Let there be light"; and there was light. (Gen. 1:3)

> Then God said, "Let there be a firmament in the midst of the waters…" (Gen. 1:6)
>
> Then God said, "Let the waters under the heavens be gathered together…" (Gen. 1:9)
>
> Then God said, "Let the earth bring forth grass, the herb…" (Gen. 1:11)
>
> Then God said, "Let there be lights in the firmament of the heavens to divide the day from night…" (Gen. 1:14)
>
> Then God said, "Let the waters abound with an abundance of living creatures…" (Gen. 1:20)
>
> Then God said, "Let the earth bring forth living creatures according to its kind…" (Gen. 1:24)
>
> Then God said, "Let Us make man in Our image, according to Our likeness…" (Gen. 1:26)

As you see, when God spoke, things were created; it was by His Word that things were made. Not once does it say that He made anything with His hands. He spoke; it was by His Logos that things were made and created. It's by the living Word of God that we came into existence, and we were made in His image according to His likeness. The Word of God is an essential part of our very being and without it we have no life.

Rhema

> All flesh is as grass, and all the glory of man as the flower of the grass. The grass withers, and its flower falls away, but the word of the LORD endures forever. (Isa. 40:6–8)

Now this is the word which by the gospel was preached to you. (1 Pet. 1:24–25)

Here Peter repeats what is told by Isaiah, that the Word of the Lord endures forever; it is everlasting. That man and his glory will wither and fade away as quickly as the grass, but the Word of God endures forever. And this is the very word that is preached through the gospels of Jesus the Christ. You see, we need the Word of God in us to endure forever and give us everlasting life.

Now in this passage from Peter, he speaks of the Word of God in a different form. The word he uses here in Greek is *Rhema* (hray'-mah), meaning

1. That which is or has been uttered by the living voice, thing spoken, word
    a) Any sound produced by the voice and having definite meaning
    b) Speech, discourse
        1) What one has said
    c) A series of words joined together into a sentence (a declaration of one's mind made in words)
        1) An utterance
        2) A saying of any sort as a message, a narrative 1c
            a) Concerning some occurrence
2. Subject matter of speech, thing spoken of
    a) So far forth as it is a matter of narration
    b) So far as it is a matter of command
    c) A matter of dispute, case at law

This here Peter is referring to the very words spoken by God through the Lord Jesus the Christ. John the Baptist uses the same version of the "word" as Peter when he says, "For He whom God sent speaks the words [*Rhema*] of God, for God does not give the Spirit by measure."

IF WE ARE SAVED, ARE WE PROMISED HEAVEN?

If you notice, John mentions in the same breath that whom God sent speaks the *Rhema* of God, for God doesn't give the Spirit by measure. I want to mention that the word "give" here in Greek is *didomi* (did'-o-mee), meaning

1. To give
2. To give something to someone
    a) Of one's own accord to give one something, to his advantage
        1) To bestow a gift
    b) To grant, give to one asking, let have
    c) To supply, furnish, necessary things
    d) To give over, deliver
        1) To reach out, extend, present
        2) Of a writing
        3) To give over to one's care, entrust, commit
            a) Something to be administered
            b) To give or commit to some one something to be religiously observed
    e) To give what is due or obligatory, to pay: wages or reward
    f) To furnish, endue
3. To give
    a) To cause, profuse, give forth from one's self
        1) To give, hand out lots
    b) To appoint to an office
    c) To cause to come forth, i.e. as the sea, death and Hell are said to give up the dead who have been engulfed or received by them
    d) To give one to someone as his own
        1) As an object of his saving care

2) To give one to someone, to follow him as a leader and master
3) To give one to someone to care for his interests
4) To give one to someone to whom he already belonged, to return
   a) To grant or permit one
   b) To commission

What John is saying here is that God will grant, permit, entrust, commission, give, endue, or administer His Spirit to you by the living *Rhema* from God through Jesus the Christ. The very same thing Jesus said about the Holy Spirit in John, "the Spirit of truth, whom the world cannot receive, because it neither sees Him nor knows Him" (John 14:17). Are John and the Christ Jesus telling us that it takes knowing God, His living word, and learning from Christ to be granted or commissioned the Spirit of God?

Now take note here that many say in John 3:34, John is speaking of God not giving the Spirit by measure to Christ. Don't be misled; let's think about this for a moment. Christ Jesus is part of the Trinity, what we call the Godhead, and can't be commissioned something that is already part of Him. The Holy Spirit, God, and Christ Jesus are one; they are all God. Jesus was God's Word in the flesh; the Spirit was never given to Him because it was part Him already.

Many believe that Jesus was commissioned with, or given the Holy Spirit, when He was baptized by John the Baptist in the Jordan River, because it says that the Spirit of God descended like a dove and alighted upon Him (Matt. 3:16). The baptism was only to fulfill the righteousness of prophecy; it was an outward show of God glorifying His Son and marking the beginning of His ministry. It was not God giving Jesus the Holy Spirit, because it was already part of Him. If you notice in Luke 2:46–47, Jesus was found in the temple at the age of twelve, discussing the Scripture with the teachers, and they were astonished at His understanding and answers. This knowledge and understanding shows Jesus possessed the Spirit of God and was already about His Father's business at the age of twelve (Luke 2:49). This was twenty-one years before His baptism in the Jordan River.

Receiving His Testimony

John the Baptist tells us,

> He who comes from above is above all; he who is of the earth is earthly and speaks of the earth. He who comes from heaven is above all. And what He has seen and heard, that He testifies; and no one receives His testimony. He who has received His testimony has certified that God is true. For He whom God sent speaks the words of God, for God does not give the Spirit by measure. The Father loves the Son, and has given all things into His hand. He who believes in the Son has everlasting life; and he who does not believe the Son shall not see life, but the wrath of God abides on him. (John 3:31–36)

We need God's Word to take on His Spirit; we need God's Word to truly believe. It's through His Word and testimony that we begin to believe and know God.

If you think about this, where it says, "And no one receives His testimony," is it much different today from back in the first century, during the time of Jesus? Many didn't want to receive the Lord's testimony or the things He told them, especially the religious leaders. They wanted to hold on to their own interpretation of God's Word or, back then, God's law. They didn't want hear what the Lord Jesus had to say; they were content in doing things their own way, and they didn't want to change.

Same thing today, people want to hold on to what they want to believe is God's Word and continue doing the same things they have always done; they don't want to change either. They don't want to sit down and take time to receive God's testimony and change the way they live their lives. They want to follow their own beliefs, say a magic prayer, continue living life their way, and just ask God to be forgiven in the Lord Jesus's name. Living as a Christian in this manner is not what it means to believe in Jesus, and that's not going to save you from the wrath of God.

Receiving His testimony and believing in it means that you certify that God is true and the Lord Jesus is His Son and what the Lord Jesus tells us is from God. And if you know and truly believe in God and His Son, the Lord Jesus the Christ, then you will change the way you live and follow Him. You can't truly believe in Him and not follow His commands. And without true belief in Christ and His Word, there's no everlasting life.

Take note here in this last verse:

> He who believes in the Son has everlasting life; and he who does not believe the Son shall not see life, but the wrath of God abides on him. (John 3:36)

This is a twofold statement containing two different kinds of beliefs. The first half says, "He who believes in the Son has everlasting life." This part addresses the believing in Christ Jesus. The second half says, "And he who does not believe the Son shall not see life, but the wrath of God abides on him." If you notice here it doesn't say, "He who does not believe in the Son"; it says, "He who does not believe the Son."

The Greek word for "he who does not believe" is *apeitheo* (ä-pā-the'-ō), meaning

1. Not to allow one's self to be persuaded; not to comply with;
   a) To refuse or withhold belief;
   b) To refuse belief and obedience.

And just for a little extra information: the word *apeitheo* is translated sixteen times in the Bible: eight times as believe not, four times as disobedient, three times as obey not, once as unbelieving (Strong's).

John is telling us that not only do we have to believe in Christ Jesus, but we have to be obedient to Him as well, or we will face the wrath of God. Let me put it another way: John is telling you that not only do you have to believe in Christ Jesus, but you also must comply with the vary words Jesus commands. You must believe in the Teacher, and you must do as the Teacher teaches. Or you face the consequences, and that is the wrath of God.

Learn from Him

Jesus tells us in Matthew,

> Come to Me, all you who are heavy laden, and I will give you rest. Take My yoke upon you and learn from Me, for I am gentle and lowly in heart, and you will find rest for your souls. (Matt. 11:28–29)

He tells us all of you who are struggling (and everyone is struggling; I don't know anyone who isn't) to come to Him so He can give you rest. How does He give you rest? By taking His yoke upon you and learning from Him. He gives you strength by learning from Him. The key point in this is to learn from Him, the Lord Jesus Himself. We learn from Him and come to understand the gospel by studying His Word and spending time with Him. If you do this, He will give you rest for your souls, rest from your struggles, and rest from the Lord's vengeance.

Jesus said we must take His yoke upon ourselves and learn from Him. To give you a better understanding of what Jesus is saying here about taking His yoke upon you, let me explain it in more detail. When a farmer went to plow his field, he would yoke two bulls together to pull the plow. Now when the farmer had a young new bull to train to pull the plow, the farmer would yoke it together with his leading, older, bigger, and stronger bull. A bull that was exceptionally experienced enough to train and teach the younger bull what to do. The bigger bull would also carry the load until the younger bull learned what to do and became strong enough to help plow the field.

Imagine this, God is the farmer, and this world is His field. There is a crop to be planted, and there is work to be done before the harvest, the day of judgment. Jesus is the lead bull that we as believers need to be yoked together with, in order to learn and be strengthened enough to do God's will. So at the time of harvest we can be gathered into His rest; we can be that part of the crop that is gathered into His barn, His heaven. As you see, we must be yoked together with Jesus and learn from Him to attain this rest for our souls. And in turn, we must obey His teaching, His gospel, and follow His lead to escape the Lord's vengeance and be separated from His rest. In other words, if we aren't helping Him do the work that needs to be done before the harvest, then we are in His way, and He is going to be a little upset with those hindering His work.

That's one way you can look at it, but now let's look at the actual meaning of "yoked" and apply it to how we live our lives today, and how the Lord Jesus would like us to live. The word "yoked" used here in Greek is *zugos* (dzoo-gos'), meaning

1. A yoke
    a) A yoke that is put on draught cattle
    b) Metaph., used of any burden or bondage
        1) As that of slavery
        2) Of troublesome laws imposed on one, esp. of the Mosaic law, hence the name is so transferred to the commands of Christ as to contrast them with the commands of the Pharisees which were a veritable "yoke"; yet even Christ's

>   commands must be submitted to,
>   though easier to be kept
>   2. A balance, pair of scales

So what we see here is that a yoke can be considered any burden or bondage, something that can enslave you. Maybe something such as an addiction, depression, anxiety, despair, or any emotional or mental distress that has a hold on you and you can't get free from. The Lord Jesus said come and learn from Me, submit to My authority, and take My yoke upon you; it is easy, and the burden is light.

His way will give you rest from these burdens and struggles that are weighing you down and have you trapped. His yoke will give you freedom from the yokes you struggle with in your life today.

> But now having been set free from sin, and having become slaves of God, you have your fruit to holiness, and the end, everlasting life. For the wages of sin is death, but the gift of God is eternal life in Christ Jesus our Lord. (Rom. 6:22–23)

Either way you are yoked to something in your life: you're a slave to sin (death) or a slave to Christ (life).

Bread of Life

Jesus said,

> Do not labor for the food which perishes, but for the food which endures to everlasting life, which the Son of Man will give you, because God the Father has set His seal on Him. (John 6:27)

What is Jesus telling us here, that we should labor for the food that gives everlasting life? I believe He is, because if we look back at the very first thing that the Lord Jesus teaches us, this means going to the beginning of the New Testament in the gospel of Matthew. And the first thing that is recorded or remembered that Jesus said, other than Him permitting John the Baptist to baptize Him, is when we hear Jesus, when He is tempted by Satan, say,

> It is written, "Man shall not live by bread alone, but by every word that proceeds from the mouth of God." (Matt. 4:4)

We hear Jesus telling us, and the devil, that there is nothing more important to us than the Word or *Rhema* of God. It is more important than the very food we eat. That we can't survive alone on what we call food, but by every word that proceeds from the mouth of God. Jesus tells us in the very beginning that we need the Word of God to live.

Again Jesus says,

> For the bread of God is He who comes down from heaven and gives life to the world. (John 6:33)

And again,

> I am the bread of life. He who comes to Me shall never hunger, and he who believes in Me shall never thirst. (John 6:35)

Is Jesus telling us that He is the bread and living water that gives everlasting life and that we should labor or diligently seek Him? This is exactly what Jesus is telling us. He says,

> Most assuredly, I say to you, he who believes in Me has everlasting life. I am the bread of life. (John 6:47–48)

Then Jesus goes on to explain this more in depth. He says to us,

> Most assuredly, I say to you, unless you eat the flesh of the Son of Man and drink His blood, you have no life in you. Whoever eats My flesh and drinks My blood has eternal life, and I will raise him up at the last day. For My flesh is food indeed, and My blood is drink indeed. He who eats My flesh and drinks My blood abides in Me, and I in him. As the living Father sent Me, and I live because of the Father, so he who feeds on Me will live because of Me. (John 6:53–57)

Does this sound like we can just profess that we believe in Jesus? Jesus tells us here that we must feed on Him; He said that unless we eat and drink of Him, we have no life in us. Wow, that is very profound and quite clear that unless we partake in Him, we have nothing. Unless we abide in Him, we have no life in us; we are dead. So in other words, if we don't read His Word and abide in Him, we won't have everlasting life, because the only way we obtain everlasting life is through Him, Jesus.

Peter said,

> Therefore, laying aside all malice, all deceit, hypocrisy, envy, and all evil speaking, as newborn babes, desire the pure milk of the word, that you may grow thereby. (1 Pet. 2:1–2)

What Peter is telling us is to quit living the way the world has taught us and desire the pure milk of Christ, feed upon Jesus, and allow our spirit to grow. Let me put it this way: purify your heart and crave the Word of God like a baby does milk so that your spirit may grow and have everlasting life.

Remember the saying "Got milk?" If you call yourself a Christian, let me ask you this, "Do you have the pure milk of the Word?" Are you feeding upon the Word so you can grow and begin to develop a Christlike spirit? Are you growing in Christ, or are you growing against Him? Are you feeding upon Him and allowing His Spirit to grow in you, to bring you to a point of maturity and peace? Because if you're a Christian and if you're not craving the Word of God, then you're not growing and developing your spirit to its greatest potential.

Abide in Him

Jesus tells us,

> Abide in Me, and I in you. As the branch cannot bear fruit of itself, unless it abides in the vine, neither can you, unless you abide in Me. I am the vine, you are the branches. He who abides in Me, and I in him, bears much fruit; for without Me you can do nothing. If anyone does not abide in Me, he is cast out as a branch and is withered; and they gather them and throw them into the fire, and they are burned. If you abide in Me, and My words abide in you, you will ask what you desire, and it shall be done for you. By this My Father is glorified, that you bear much fruit; so you will be My disciples. (John 15:4–8)

Jesus tells us here again that we can do nothing unless we abide in Him and His words abide in us.

You may say, "That's only so we may ask what we desire." No, we may ask what we desire only as a gift of grace, because our Lord loves to give us gifts. But that's not why we abide in Him and His words abide in us. Besides, if we abide in Him, the things we ask will coincide with His will. We abide in Him through His Word; and if we don't, we will be cast out and withered, to be thrown into the fire. You may think that I am taking this a little too far, but you will see and come to understand it more as we get deeper into His Word.

Knowing God

Now we are beginning to gain a fair understanding of what we need to do to escape the Lord's vengeance. I want to make mention of what the Lord Jesus says in the beginning of the Lord's Prayer in John 17:1–3. Jesus said,

> Father, the hour has come. Glorify Your Son, that Your Son also may glorify You, as You have given Him authority over all flesh, that He should give eternal life to as many as You have given Him. And this is eternal life, that they may know You, the only true God, and Jesus Christ whom You have sent.

You notice that Jesus makes mention of as many as God has given Him. Could this mean as many as God has yoked together with Him?

So what is eternal life? Eternal life is that you may know, let me repeat this, may KNOW God and the Lord Jesus the Christ. You only know someone and come to love him or her when and only when you spend time with him or her. The only way you can know God and the Lord Jesus is to spend time with Him and in His Word. The word "know" in Greek is *ginosko* (ghin-oce'-ko), meaning

1. To learn to know, come to know, get a knowledge of, perceive, feel
   a) To become known
2. To know, understand, perceive, have knowledge of
   a) To understand
   b) To know
3. Jewish idiom for sexual intercourse between a man and a woman
4. To become acquainted with, to know

What the Lord Jesus is saying here is that eternal life comes by having a close relationship with God. Learning about Him, obtaining knowledge of Him to the point of a deep inner connection, becoming acquainted with God. He wants you to perceive and understand Him to the point of a deep inner loving relationship with Him. Are you starting to get the picture here? Eternal life comes by knowing and loving God and the Lord Jesus the Christ, and we must learn from Jesus if we want to go to heaven. God wants your attention. He is looking for your heart, to see if you truly know Him and love Him.

Paul writes,

> But then, indeed, when you did not know God,
> you served those which by nature are not gods.
> (Gal. 4:8)

Here Paul uses a different word for "know." This word is *eido* (ā'-dō), meaning

1. To see
    a) To perceive with the eyes
    b) To perceive by any of the senses
    c) To perceive, notice, discern, discover
    d) To see
        1) i.e. to turn the eyes, the mind, the attention to anything
        2) To pay attention, observe
        3) To see about something
            a) i.e. to ascertain what must be done about it
        4) To inspect, examine
        5) To look at, behold
    e) To experience any state or condition
    f) To see, i.e. have an interview with, to visit
2. To know
    a) To know of anything

    b) To know, i.e. get knowledge of, understand, perceive
       1) Of any fact
       2) The force and meaning of something which has definite meaning
       3) To know how, to be skilled in
    c) To have regard for one, cherish, pay attention to

Paul says here that when you don't know God, you serve the very nature of things other than God: this world, your flesh, and your ego. Paul is telling us that if we don't get knowledge of, understand, pay attention to, and observe God, to the point that we ascertain what must be done, then we won't be able to follow Him.

What you have to ask yourself here is how do you live today? As a Christian, a son of God, what is it that you serve? Do you live for yourself and the things that you desire to have and do?

As an example, some people love their car or truck. They spend every weekend washing it and waxing it, taking time to clean every detail on the inside. They polish the rims up real nice and apply a protecting sealer on the seats and dashboard. They do all this work themselves, making sure every detail is done perfect and to their expectations. They make sure the best oil is used and changed often; the very best gas that is available is used as well. They treasure their vehicle with all their heart and make sure it gets the best care and attention possible. Some people are like this with sports, music, their jobs, their looks, their homes, everything but God. They serve themselves and whatever they own, more so than the One who made them possible.

What are the things that you idolize and put before God, and why is that? Is it only because you don't know God, or you think you do but have a misconception of Him because you don't spend time getting to really know Him by reading His Word? These are serious questions you need to ask yourself, especially if you have asked Jesus to come into your heart and be your Lord and Savior and you haven't seen a significant change in your life: how you think, how you act, and who you are.

Paul presses on to really drive this into the reader's heart by following it up with the following:

> But now after you have known God, or rather are known by God, how is it that you turn again to the weak and beggarly elements, to which you desire again to be in bondage? (Gal. 4:9)

Paul tells us that after we have known God, how is it that we return to serving the same things we idolized before we knew God? He talks about turning again to the same burdens and struggles we were previously yoked to, the very things that enslaved us.

> Stand fast therefore in the liberty by which Christ has made us free, and do not be entangled again with a yoke of bondage. (Gal. 5:1)

Submerge yourself in Christ, take His yoke upon you, and learn from Him (Matt. 11:29). Read His Word and get to know Him. Allow His Spirit to come upon you and change your heart so that you may have freedom and rest.

> I say then: Walk in the Spirit, and you shall not fulfill the lust of the flesh. For the flesh lusts against the Spirit, and the Spirit against the flesh; and these are contrary to one another, so that you do not do the things that you wish. (Gal. 5:16–17)

You see that when you are filled with the Spirit, you follow the will of the Lord, not your own. Do you think this change is automatic, that it comes magically upon us? No, it doesn't. It takes time. It takes your attention. It takes you loving Jesus to allow His Spirit to work in your heart and change you.

Spirit and Truth

For when your heart is truly for something, you give your all to attain it. So I ask you this, "Is your heart truly for God?" For Jesus said when He was talking to the Samaritan woman,

> You worship what you do not know; we know what we worship, for salvation is of the Jews. But the hour is coming, and now is, when the true worshipers will worship the Father in spirit and truth; for the Father is seeking such to worship Him. God is Spirit, and those who worship Him must worship in spirit and truth. (John 4:22–24)

Just as the Samaritans back then, many people today worship what they do not know.

Many people think they know God and His Word; they go off what others tell them and have never read the Bible. They say a magic prayer and go to church once a week, they continue to live their lives as they always have, but now they say, "All I have to do is ask to be forgiven and I'm okay. God made me the way I am, and He knows what I will do. All I have to do is ask for forgiveness. His Word says so, so I'm good." The truth is that they are wrong and don't know what they are talking about, because they don't know God. Jesus says that the true worshippers will worship in spirit and truth. This means is your spirit TRULY for God? Do you truly worship Him with all your heart? Do you take the time to get to know Him and what His Word truly says?

Let me just tell you now, God didn't make people the way they are today; the world has. God did create each of us individually, with different traits, personalities, characteristics, and talents. But He didn't create mankind to think the way they do today; the world has done this. You think and act the way you do from all the things you have been taught since your birth; this has made you who you are, not God. And God wants to change you to who you were meant to be when He created you, but you have to make that conscious effort to learn from Him to allow this change to happen.

Jesus said,

> The first of all the commandments is; "Hear, O Israel, the Lord our God, the Lord is one. And you shall love the Lord your God with all your heart, with all your soul, with all your mind, and with all your strength." This is the first commandment. (Mark 12:29–30)

The key points here are all your HEART, all your SOUL, your entire MIND, and all your STRENGTH. You get that? You are to love God with everything you got and do it with all your might.

Living for Christ

In John 12, Jesus has dinner with Lazarus in Bethany, and then the next day He goes to Jerusalem riding on the donkey's colt. Now shortly after His arrival, some Greeks came to see Jesus. They approached Philip asking for Jesus, Philip went to Andrew, and in turn Andrew and Philip told Jesus (John 12:22). Jesus answers them, saying,

> The hour has come that the Son of Man should be glorified. Most assuredly, I say to you, unless a grain of wheat falls into the ground and dies, it remains alone; but if it dies, it produces much grain. (John 12:23–24)

Just a thought here, when Jesus mentions the grain, is He speaking only of Himself and what His crucifixion will produce or of us too and our selfish spirit? I say this because if we keep our selfish attitude and only care of ourselves, won't we possibly die alone? And if we put to death our selfish spirit and become Christlike, taking on the Spirit of Christ, do we not love others and bring glory to Christ, producing much more people to do the same?

Then Jesus continues to say,

> He who loves his life will lose it, and he who hates his life in this world will keep it for eternal life. If anyone serves Me, let him follow Me; and where I am, there My servant will be also. If anyone serves Me, him My Father will honor. (John 12:25–26)

I find this interesting that Jesus would bring this issue up at a time when the Greeks, or Gentiles, are seeking to see Him. He tells those who wish to follow Him, they must forsake their lives for Him and the gospel in order to gain life. Is that eternal life? And the one who loves their life and only lives for their self will lose it, that they will only die?

Right after Jesus says this, in the very same breath, He talks of following Him and serving Him. You see, when you make Jesus your Lord, you have to surrender your life to Him, to follow Him and serve Him. You don't continue living your life the way you want to live it; you live the way He wants you to live. He tells us that when we serve Him, God the Father will honor us.

So when we call upon Jesus to be our Lord and Savior, we must take account of the way we are living and make changes. Jesus says,

> I have come as a light into the world, that whoever believes in Me should not abide in darkness. (John 12:46)

He tells us that if we believe in Him, we shouldn't continue to abide in darkness, which means we were abiding in darkness by the way we were living before He came into our hearts, and that we shouldn't continue living that way any longer. We are to walk in His light, and His light is to shine through us by the way we live.

Then Jesus goes on to say,

> And if anyone hears My words and does not believe, I do not judge him; for I did not come to judge the world but to save the world. He who rejects Me, and does not receive My words, has that which judges him—the word that which I have spoken will judge him in that last day. (John 12:47–48)

So what Jesus is saying here is that He didn't come to judge you but to give you knowledge that will save you on that last day, giving you everlasting life.

But if you don't follow what He tells you by taking His words to heart—that is, believing in them—then it will be the very words you didn't follow that you will be judged by in the last day, the day of judgment. Could this be why Jesus said that some shall not taste death until they see Him coming in His kingdom? Could this mean that because some don't take His words to heart and believe in them, they don't really have everlasting life?

Jesus continues,

> For I have not spoken on My own authority; but the Father who sent Me gave Me a command, what I should say and what I should speak. And I know that His command is everlasting life. Therefore, whatever I speak, just as the Father has told Me, so I speak. (John 12:49–50)

Now Jesus tells us that these are the very words that we are to follow, and these are straight from God the Father Himself. These words are God's command. And God's command, or God's Word, is everlasting life.

Denying Oneself

One of the hardest things Jesus tells His followers to do is that one must forsake his life to gain it. Now this is where it gets deep. In Matthew 16, Jesus said to His disciples (that is, everyone who follows Jesus and learns from Him),

> If anyone desires to come after Me, let him deny himself, and take up his cross and follow Me. For whoever desires to save his life will lose it, but whoever loses his life for My sake will find it. For what profit is it to a man if he gains the whole world, and loses his own soul? Or what will a man give in exchange for his soul? (Matt. 16:24–26)

Let me stop here for a moment. In verse 24, Jesus says we must—MUST—deny ourselves and follow Him.

In a society where everything is about self—what you have, what you have done, your success, how much money you make, who you are, who you know, who knows you—you must deny it all and put Jesus first. That means put Jesus and God before everything you know. Then Jesus says what will you give, you GIVE, in exchange for your soul. In other words, what will you give in exchange for eternal life? Will you put the material things of this world before God? Do you worship what you have or who you are? One must truly ask themselves these questions if they intend to enter the kingdom of heaven. He says whoever loses his life will find it. If you lose your material life, you will find your eternal life.

And I know some of you are saying at this moment, "Yeah right, I have kids and a family who depend on me, bills to pay, etc." I understand this; I have kids and bills too. The Lord Jesus understands this as well, and so does God. Jesus said,

> Therefore do not worry, saying, "What shall we eat?" or "What shall we drink?" or "What shall

> we wear?" For all these things the Gentiles seek. For your heavenly Father knows that you need all these things. But seek first the kingdom of God and His righteousness, and all these things shall be added to you. (Matthew 6:31–33)

God knows you have bills to pay and a family to feed. Just put Him and His righteousness first in your life and He will make sure you have the ability to meet all your needs.

Not only that, Jesus also tells us,

> Assuredly, I say to you, there is no one who has left house or brothers or sisters or father or mother or children or lands, for My sake and the gospel's, who shall not receive a hundred fold now in this time—houses and brothers and sisters and mothers and children and lands, with persecutions—and in the age to come, eternal life. (Mark 10:29–30)

What Jesus is telling us is that everything we lose in our life for following Him and the gospel, He will give us back a hundredfold, now and in the life to come. That's a promise that can't be beaten by anything in this world. What a blessing Jesus promises us if we deny our way of living for His, take up our cross, and crucify our evil nature, for Him and the gospel; that whatever we lose for doing so, He will return a hundredfold.

Don't take this the wrong way, thinking that you are to quit your job, leave your wife and kids, and go out into the street and start preaching, "Jesus saves," expecting the Lord to give you a hundredfold for doing so. What Jesus is telling you here is to quit living your life for yourself and to start living it for Him. That you are to learn from Him and follow His way of living and put His principles into practice. That if you do this and whatever you lose for doing so, He will return a hundredfold.

Jesus can make this promise because He knows that if you put God first and His principles into practice, the only things you stand to lose are those that aren't good for you anyway. Your job or career will flourish and prosper, or possibly your path will change and you find a better one. Your relationships will become stronger and more loving, and the ones that are broken will be healed. Your perception will change from the things you once thought were really important in your life toward the things that are truly important in your life.

Understand this though, it is going to take some effort to deny ourselves and change the way we live in order to follow the Lord Jesus and His gospel. Our egos can be a very powerful force to overcome, especially when this world entices and promotes everything to improve oneself. And then you will have to endure persecutions—from this world because you are going against its way of living and from the devil because he is going to want to rob you of the blessing that is promised. And it is going to take a little effort on your part to learn from Jesus and love God.

He Promises

Jesus goes,

> For the Son of Man will come in the glory of His Father with His angels, and then He will reward each according to his works. Assuredly, I say to you, there are some standing here who shall not taste death till they see the Son of Man coming in His kingdom. (Matt. 16:27–28)

This is very interesting, and one should take note of what is said here. Jesus very clearly says first you must deny yourself and follow Him, then asks what you are willing to give up for eternal life and follows it up with the fact that He is coming with rewards.

What is He going to reward? He is going to reward each person according to his works. That's right, you read that right, your works.

He is going to reward you for your works. I'm not saying you work to earn your salvation; that is far from what the Scripture says. Our salvation comes by the grace of God through our belief in Christ, but our rewards or blessings come from how we act on our faith and belief. Jesus says He is going to reward us for our works, the things we do when following Him. And believe me it takes work to follow Jesus, to make a conscious effort to change our ways to be Christlike, to be a Christian.

Keep in mind here, Jesus said, "Assuredly I say to you." When Jesus says this, He is making you a promise that what He says is the truth, and it cannot be broken. I repeat, cannot be broken. Jesus promises that there are some who will not taste death until He comes in His kingdom. Now, it is clear He is talking to His disciples here, not the crowds or the people in general. These are His chosen followers, the ones who call Him Lord. These are the ones who are called to learn from Him. These are the saved! It is very simple: if you call upon Jesus and ask Him to be your Lord and Savior, you surrender your life to Him and follow Him and learn from Him.

And Jesus says that some will not taste death until He comes with His kingdom, the kingdom of heaven. Could this mean the second death? I believe it could be, especially since Jesus doesn't recognize death. He continuously says that people are only sleeping and are not dead throughout His ministry. The only death He recognizes is the second death at the time of the great white throne judgment, when God's wrath or vengeance is revealed.

Many believe that because Jesus had said this to His disciples right before the transfiguration on the mountain, He was speaking of His glory that will be shown on the mountain. I don't necessarily agree with this teaching because when Jesus had said this, He was in the middle of talking about when He comes in His kingdom, about the time of His return in all His glory with His angels, the end of days.

Now this is a very profound thing to say to His disciples. Jesus said that some would not taste death until He comes with His kingdom. Could this mean that some of His disciples are going to be judged and die; could that mean some who say they are Christians and call Jesus Lord are going to be judged and die? Believe this, if He will say this to His disciples, those who were close to Him, He will say the same to those who call themselves believers today.

I believe Jesus said this because some didn't truly believe in Him, and it's the same today. There's more to just professing your faith and belief; it must come from the heart. If you don't truly believe in your heart and have faith in Christ, then you truly aren't saved. This is something to think seriously about when we look at how we live our lives, because if you truly believe, your life would portray it.

As you may start to see and understand, the importance of learning God's Word and the gospel of our Lord Jesus the Christ is a very significant part of obtaining eternal life. It not only plays an important part of obtaining eternal life, but also determines where we stand with God on that day of judgment, whether we truly believe or not. My suggestion to you is get to know God, learn His Word, learn the gospel, and learn from Christ Jesus, our Lord and Savior; take the first step to everlasting life.

3

Becoming a New Creation

> Since you have purified your souls in obeying the truth through the Spirit in sincere love of the brethren, love one another fervently with a pure heart, having been born again, not of corruptible seed but incorruptible, through the word of God which lives and abides forever.
>
> —1 Peter 1:22–23

Many believe that it's God's Spirit that changes the heart, that it is His Spirit that makes us new. This is true in a sense; His Spirit makes us a new creation, but only by helping us change. As I said before, God takes us at our word when we confess Jesus to be our Lord and Savior; so He sends us a helper, the Holy Spirit. Jesus said,

> Nevertheless I tell you the truth. It is to your advantage that I go away; for if I do not go away, the Helper will not come to you; but if I depart, I will send Him to you. (John 16:7)

Jesus left this world so He can send us the Helper, to assist us in the process of conversion or to be reborn.

You hear it quoted quite often,

> Therefore, if anyone is in Christ, he is a new creation; old things have passed away; behold, all things have become new. (2 Cor. 5:17)

They often quote this scripture after a person has just been baptized. They tell them they're a new creation now and that they've been made new. But the person doesn't feel any different, so some believe they are different, and some don't. Thus, they continue living their life the same way they always have. What a misconception of this scripture. No wonder many people fail to change and never become a true Christian. They never actually become born again. This scripture tells us, "If anyone is in Christ, he is a new creation." That means we have to be in Christ; we must abide in Him. How do we abide in Christ? We eat of His flesh and drink of His blood. In other words, we read His Word; we follow His will and do as He commands; we take His yoke upon us and learn from Him. This is what makes us a new creation, not just saying some words out of our mouth.

Born Again

We take God at His Word. If the Bible says it, it must be true. So God takes us at our word as well. If we profess with our mouth that we believe in our heart that He raised Jesus from the dead and that we ask Jesus to come into our hearts to be our Lord and Savior, then He gives us a new Spirit. This is what many call being born again.

Many believe that we say this magic prayer and we are saved, that we are good to go and we are going to heaven. I hear it said quite often after a person accepts Jesus to be their Lord and Savior, "Now you have fire insurance. You're going to heaven." And that is about the most deceiving thing that can be said to a new believer. What a new believer should be told is that they have just made a commitment to Jesus as their Lord and now need to spend some time reading their Bible and getting to know God. They should be told that they have just taken the first step toward going to heaven.

So let's see what Jesus says about being born again. There was a man of the Pharisees named Nicodemus, a member of the Jewish ruling council. This man came to Jesus by night saying,

> Rabbi, we know that You are a teacher come from God; for no one can do these signs that You do unless God is with him. (John 3:1–2)

Jesus replied,

> Most assuredly, I say to you, unless one is born again, he cannot see the kingdom of God. (John 3: 3)

Then after, Nicodemus asks how a man can be born again when he is old and how one can enter the womb a second time. Jesus repeats Himself, but this time with more depth. Jesus answered,

> Most assuredly, I say to you, unless one is born of water and the Spirit, he cannot enter the kingdom of God. (John 3:5)

Now here in John 3:5, many believe that Jesus is saying that one must be baptized in water to be born again. It is interesting to note, if you look up the words in John 3:5 in Greek, the language the New Testament was written, the word for born in Greek is *gennao* (ghen-nah'-o), meaning

1. of men who fathered children
    a) to be born
    b) to be begotten

                1) of women giving birth to children
    2. metaph.
        a) to engender, cause to arise, excite
        b) in a Jewish sense, of one who brings others over to his way of life, to convert someone
        c) of God making Christ his son
        d) of God making men His sons through faith in Christ's work

It is interesting that the definition of "born" in a Jewish sense has a meaning of one who brings others over to his way of life, to convert someone. It's the definition of God making men His sons through faith in Christ's work. Then the very next word after *gennao* is *ejk* (ek), meaning out of, from, by, away from.

So the literal meaning in Greek could be "born out of," "begotten from," or "engender by" water and Spirit. But the Jewish sense is "being converted by" or "converted from" water and Spirit. Now we should use the Jewish sense of this because Jesus, who said it, was a Jew and John, who wrote it, was a Jew. So in a sense, what we have here is Jesus saying that unless one is converted or brought over to His way of life by water and Spirit, he cannot enter the kingdom of God. Is Jesus saying that being born again means one must be converted to His way of living by water and Spirit?

Water and Spirit

What does Jesus mean by being born of, or converted from, water and Spirit? Does water here mean baptism? I don't believe so, because if you read a little further in John, in chapter 4, Jesus speaks of water again. When Jesus is with the Samaritan woman, He talks of living water.

> If you knew the gift of God, and who it is who says to you, "Give Me a drink," you would have

asked Him, and He would have given you living
water. (John 4:10)

Then a few moments later Jesus says,

But whoever drinks of the water that I shall give
him will never thirst. But the water that I shall
give him will become in him a fountain of water
springing up into everlasting life. (John 4:14)

And a little later on you find Jesus stood and cried out, saying,

If anyone thirsts, let him come to Me and drink.
He who believes in Me, as the Scripture has said,
out of his heart will flow rivers of living water.
(John 7:37–38)

Then John tells us,

But this He spoke concerning the Spirit, whom
those believing in Him would receive; for the
Holy Spirit was not yet given, because Jesus was
not yet glorified. (John 7:39)

In this last scripture, John 7:39, John is telling us that Jesus is referring to the Holy Spirit when He mentions living water. Now if we go back to John 3:5 and take a look at the word "and" in Greek, it is *kaiv* (kahee), meaning and, even, also, indeed, but.

So the scripture could say "born from water even Spirit" or "converted to a new way of living from water even Spirit." If we take into consideration what John tells us the meaning of what Jesus meant by water and the Greek translation to the word "and," we can see that water and Spirit are considerably the same. But if this were the case, why wouldn't Jesus just say Spirit? Why make mention of both?

I believe Jesus says "water and Spirit" because we need something more than just His Spirit to be born again. Jesus gave living water through the words He spoke. He said those who come and drink from Me, those who come to Me and listen to My words and digest them in their heart, out of them will flow rivers of living water. Jesus spoke of water meaning the Word of God, because it's through the Word of God you gain His Spirit. And when your heart is filled with the Word and Spirit, you become changed; you become born again and converted to a new way of living.

We need His Word, and to believe in Him, we have to have faith that what He says is true. Even the apostles knew they needed something more. They said to the Lord,

Increase our faith. (Luke 17:5)

When they said that, Jesus spoke to them. It was by His words and what He told them that increased their faith.

The apostle Peter understood the meaning of being born again. He wrote about it in his letter to the churches.

> Since you have purified your souls in obeying the truth through the Spirit in sincere love of the brethren, love one another fervently with a pure heart, having been born again, not of corruptible seed but incorruptible, through the word of God which lives and abides forever. (1 Pet. 1:22–23)

Peter said it, "having been born again, through the word of God." It is by His Word that we are changed; it is by the Word of God that we take on a Christlike Spirit.

Receiving His Spirit

We can't change our spirit by just saying some words; God changes our spirit by us reading His Word. Let me say that again:

We can't change our spirit by just saying some words; God changes our spirit by us reading His Word! Our spirit is changed (born again) from reading His Word (His living water), and He sends us His Holy Spirit to help us go through this change. But look closely at what Jesus said:

> If you love Me, keep My commandments. And I will pray the Father, and He will give you another Helper, that He may abide with you forever—the Spirit of truth, whom the world cannot receive, because it neither sees Him nor knows Him, for He dwells with you and will be in you. (John 14:15–17)

Wow, Jesus tells us if we love Him to do as He says, and He will pray that the Father will give us the Holy Spirit to help us. But in the same breath Jesus tells us the world cannot receive Him because the world doesn't know Him. He tells us the Spirit dwells with us and will be in us, but does this mean first we need to know Him in order to receive Him? The only way you are going to know God's Spirit is to read God's Word.

How can we truly believe and have faith if we don't listen to Him, to the Lord Jesus? I believe we can go to church and listen to what the pastor tells us until the day we die, but it's not going to be enough to get us into heaven, because the pastor is only a man. The pastor may be telling you what the Bible says, reading passages and scriptures to you, and that is great. But it's not until you sit down with God and His Word and study it for yourself that you truly get to know God and feed your spirit. We need to take time getting to know God and His Word to truly believe and take on His Spirit!

Baptized in Christ

Hopefully by now you are starting to understand the importance of God's Word and Spirit is to being born again and that a person can't be born again without them. Now let's take a look at baptism and being baptized in Christ. And yes, I said that as if "baptism" and "baptized in Christ" are two separate things, because they are. Being baptized is a twofold process that is very important to being born again. Then there is a third element, one that is widely neglected in many of the churches today, and that is being baptized with the Holy Spirit.

Many will dispute me on this, claiming I am wrong here. They will say there is only one baptism, and once you're baptized, you are born again. They will quote what Paul says in the letter to Ephesus, "one Lord, one faith, one baptism" (Eph. 4:5). The funny thing is, the ones who will make this claim are the ones who don't really know God and His Word. You will come to realize that all three are actually a process of one baptism. Just a quick thought here: If God is a Trinity in one, and baptism came from God, to make you reborn to a new creation for God, what's to say the process isn't a Trinity in one? So I will go over all three of these, and hopefully you will see the true meaning of being baptized and born again by water and spirit.

Let's start with baptism—the baptism of repentance. This is the ceremonial act or rite of baptism performed by all the Christian churches, proclaiming the believer's rebirth. This is when a person is baptized in water, publicly announcing their belief and faith in Christ Jesus to the church and Christ. The act of being immersed in water, putting to death their former self, being born again to walk in a new life for Christ. Paul spoke of this in his letter to the Romans, in which I will get to in a moment.

First, one may say here, the baptism of repentance was the baptism given by John the Baptist to the Jews before they knew of Jesus. This is true, and isn't it the same baptism given to many Christians in the church today before they truly know Jesus? Not all, but most; some are baptized after they have a good understanding of who Christ is and what it means to follow Him. I mean most have an ideology of who Jesus is, and they want to be saved and go to heaven, but do they fully understand what it means to forsake their old way of living and follow His? Of course not. This is why it is a baptism of repentance and only the beginning or first step in being fully baptized in Christ.

Take a look at the meaning of the word "baptism" in Greek, *baptisma* (bä'p-tē-smä), meaning

> 1. Immersion, submersion
>   a) of John's baptism, that purification rite by which men on confessing their sins were bound to spiritual reformation, obtained the pardon of their past sins and became qualified for the benefits of the Messiah's kingdom soon to be set up. This was valid Christian baptism, as this was the only baptism the apostles received and it is not recorded anywhere that they were ever re-baptized after Pentecost.
>   b) of Christian baptism; a rite of immersion in water as commanded by Christ, by which one after confessing his sins and professing his faith in Christ, having been born again by the Holy Spirit unto a new life, identifies publicly with the fellowship of Christ and the church.

So what we have here is the rite, the ceremonial act, or the customary observance of baptism performed by the church, for the believer to publicly announce their belief and faith in Christ Jesus. Many believe their baptism is done after this baptism is performed, when in fact it has just begun.

Remember I said earlier that being baptized is a twofold process, meaning that it has two parts that are hinged together to make one. I have gone over the first half, the rite of baptism. Now let's go over the second half, what it means to be "baptized in Christ."

> For as many of you as were baptized into Christ have put on Christ. (Gal. 3:27)

Let's look at the word "baptized" so we may get a full understanding of baptized into Christ. The word "baptized" in Greek is *baptizo* (bap-tid'-zo), meaning

1. To dip repeatedly, to immerse, to submerge (of vessels sunk)
2. To cleanse by dipping or submerging, to wash, to make clean with water, to wash one's self, bathe
3. To overwhelm

This word is not to be confused with the root word "bapto."

> The clearest example that shows the meaning of baptizo is a text from the Greek poet and physician Nicander, who lived about 200 BC. It is a recipe for making pickles and is helpful because it uses both words. Nicander says that in order to make a pickle, the vegetable should first be "dipped" (bapto) into boiling water and then "baptized" (baptizo) in the vinegar solution. Both verbs concern the immersing of vegetables in a solution. But the first is temporary. The second, the act of baptizing the vegetable, produces a permanent change. When used in the New Testament, this word more often refers to our union and identification with Christ than to our water baptism. e.g. Mark 16:16. "He that believes and is baptized shall be saved." Christ is saying that mere intellectual ascent is not enough. There must be a union with him, a real change, like the vegetable to the pickle! (James Montgomery Boice, *Bible Study Magazine,* May 1989)

You can see here that to be baptized into Christ isn't just a mere outward show of expression by getting into a tank of water and being baptized in front of a bunch of people or just saying a confession of belief. To be baptized into Christ, you must repeatedly submerge yourself into Him to the point of being overwhelmed; you must unite yourself to Him by abiding in Him and partaking of Him. It is a process where you have to spend time getting to know Him, by reading His Word daily, calling out to Him in prayer continuously, having faith in Him always, trusting Him in everything, LOVING on Him, BELIEVING in Him.

That is submerging yourself in Christ. And when you do this, He changes you, He changes your heart, and He changes your spirit. You become a new person, a new creation in Christ Jesus; He pours out His Spirit into you, and you become Christlike and born again. This is what Paul meant in his letter to the Romans when he said,

> I beseech you brethren, by the mercies of God, that you present your bodies a living sacrifice (baptism), holy, acceptable to God, which is your reasonable service. And do not be conformed to this world, but be transformed (born again) by the renewing (baptizing) of your mind, that you may prove what is that good and acceptable and perfect will of God. (Rom. 12:1–2)

Also take note here, baptism is a noun (a thing), and baptized is a verb (an action). In other words, if you do the thing (baptism), then you must do the action (baptized in Christ). Or put it this way: if you take in the Spirit, and you don't feed the Spirit (read the Word), and you don't exercise the Spirit, then the Spirit can't grow.

Now let's talk about what I believe is the most neglected baptism in the Christian church today, the baptism of the Holy Spirit. I also believe that it is because of this neglect that the body of Christ (the church) isn't displaying the true power of God. This is why we don't see the miracles and supernatural healings in the church today, as was displayed in the first-century church. People don't believe in the supernatural powers of God because it isn't taught and shown in the churches today. It's like displaying the supernatural powers of

God during service in church is taboo in most churches, not all, but even one is too many.

If you are to believe in Christ Jesus and truly believe in your heart that He has risen from death, in order to be saved, then you are to believe in the supernatural power of God to do so. As it is written,

> If you confess with your mouth the Lord Jesus and believe in your heart that God has raised Him from the dead, you will be saved. (Rom. 10:9)

You see, you have to believe in your heart—that is, truly believe—in the supernatural abilities and power of God, Christ Jesus, and the Holy Spirit in order to be saved. You then have to believe in the supernatural ability of God to supernaturally give you a new spirit, which supernaturally makes you reborn to a new creation. And if this is so, then you have to believe that the Holy Spirit has the supernatural power to bestow supernatural gifts to those who possess the Holy Spirit within them.

So if you truly believe in the supernatural power of God, then you should want to possess the supernatural gifts and power of the Holy Spirit. And the cool thing is God wants to give you these gifts. God wants you to have them and use them to strengthen the body of Christ, for His glory. Jesus said,

> But you shall receive power when the Holy Spirit has come upon you; and you shall be witnesses to Me in Jerusalem, and in all Judea and Samaria, and to the end of the earth. (Acts 1:8)

You shall receive power, and all you have to do is believe in the supernatural power of God and ask to be baptized with His Holy Spirit.

We learn that being baptized with the Holy Spirit is separate from being baptized in the name of the Lord Jesus, in the book of Acts. In chapter 8, starting at verse 14, it is written,

> Now when the apostles who were at Jerusalem heard that Samaria had received the word of God, they sent Peter and John to them, who, when they had come down, prayed for them that they might receive the Holy Spirit. For as yet He had fallen upon none of them. They had only been baptized in the name of the Lord Jesus. Then they laid hands on them, and they received the Holy Spirit. (Acts 8:14–17)

You learn several things in these few verses. To start, those in Samaria had first received the Word of God. They had been baptized in the name of the Lord Jesus. Then you will notice that Peter and John prayed for them that they might receive the Holy Spirit. You also learn that even though they had been baptized in the name of the Lord Jesus, the Holy Spirit had not yet fallen upon them. And lastly you learn that they received the Holy Spirit by the laying on of hands by those who had already been given the Holy Spirit.

After the day of Pentecost, when the apostles were filled with the Holy Spirit, Peter gave a great sermon that cut to the heart of the people. The people then asked Peter and the rest of the apostles, what then should they do? Then Peter said to them,

> Repent, and let every one of you be baptized in the name of Jesus Christ for the remission of sins; and you shall receive the gift of the Holy Spirit. (Acts 2:38)

Peter doesn't say, "Be baptized and you will be filled with the Holy Spirit." He said, "And you shall receive." The Greek word used here for "you shall receive" is *lambano* (läm-bä'-nō), a verb meaning

1. To take
   a) To take with the hand, lay hold of, any person of thing in order to use it
      1) To take up a thing to be carried
      2) To take upon one's self
   b) To take in order to carry away
      1) Without the notion of violence, i.e. to remove, take away
   c) To take what is one's own, to take to one's self, to make one's own
      1) To claim, procure, for one's self
         a) To associate with one's self as companion, attendant
      2) Of that which when taken is not let go, to seize, lay hold of, apprehend
      3) To take by craft (our catch, used of hunters, fishermen, etc.) to circumvent one by fraud
      4) To take to one's self, lay hold upon, take possession of, i.e. to appropriate to one's self
      5) Catch at, reach after, strive to obtain
      6) To take a thing due, to collect, gather (tribute)
   d) To take
      1) To admit, receive
      2) To receive what is offered
      3) Not to refuse of reject
      4) To receive a person, give him access to one's self
         a) To regard any one's power, rank, external circumstances, and on that account to do some injustice or neglect something

      e) To take, to choose, select
      f) To take beginning, to prove anything, to make a trial of, to experience
2. To receive (what is given), to gain, get, obtain, to get back

What Peter told them was "Repent, be baptized in the name of Jesus Christ, and take hold of or claim the gift of the Holy Spirit." That is why the translation says, "You shall receive." This is clearly an action meant for one to do; it's not done for them. The Holy Spirit is for the believer to take hold of, strive for, or claim for one's self. People aren't taught this in most churches, so they are left lacking the true power of God in their lives, often failing to experience the true change meant for their spirit and life.

Many believe that the moment they are baptized in water, they are filled with the Holy Spirit and reborn. When in actuality, what they have done has been washed clean of their sins and put to death their former self, making a proclamation before the church and to Jesus that they will live their life from that moment on following Him as their Lord and Savior. In essence, what you have done is cleansed the vessel; and from that moment, what you fill it with and use it for is entirely up to you.

Am I saying that an individual isn't changed at all during baptism? No, that isn't what I'm saying. What I am saying is that during baptism, the person is cleansed, purified with a clean heart and spirit. What they do with their clean heart and spirit is entirely up to them. And from that moment, if they start to fill their heart and spirit with the Word of God, receive the gift of the Holy Spirit, and follow the Lord Jesus, then they will walk in the Spirit of God. If they don't, then they will continue to follow the flesh and walk in the spirit of this world. If they were told this before their baptism and taught correctly by the church, then I'm sure you would see a significant change in both, the believer and the church.

The Spirit

Now that we are gaining some understanding how important the Word of God is in being reborn and given His Spirit, let's go back to John 3 where Jesus is talking about being born again. Right after He tells us we must be born of water or by the Word and Spirit, Jesus said,

> That which is born of the flesh is flesh, and that which is born of the Spirit is spirit. Do not marvel that I said to you, "You must be born again." The wind blows where it wishes, and you hear the sound of it, but cannot tell where it comes from and where it goes. So is everyone who is born of the Spirit. (John 3:6–8)

The Spirit plays a very important role in being born again and our salvation. Jesus tells us how important the Spirit is when He was speaking with the Samaritan woman at the well. Jesus said,

> But the hour is coming, and now is, when the true worshipers will worship the Father in spirit and truth; for the Father is seeking such to worship Him. God is Spirit, and those who worship Him must worship in spirit and truth. (John 4:23–24)

So as you see, God is seeking those who are going to truly worship Him in spirit. God is Spirit, so we must worship in spirit—spirit and truth.

Now if we must worship God in spirit and truth, can we just say this magic prayer and we're good to go? Is it that easy? I don't believe it is. Otherwise, Jesus wouldn't have said,

> Strive to enter through the narrow gate, for many, I say to you, will seek to enter and will not be able. (Luke 13:24)

Jesus tells us,

> If anyone loves Me, he will keep My word; and My Father will love him, and We will come to him and make Our home with him. He who does not love Me does not keep My words; and the word which you hear is not Mine but the Father's who sent Me. (John 14:23–24)

It is quite clear that if we love Him and keep His Word, the Lord Jesus and the Father will come and make Their home with us. You catch that? That if we keep His words and love Him, again I say that it is through keeping His words and by loving Him, that They come to make Their home with us. Here we have Jesus telling us again that it is when we keep His words that we gain His Spirit. What Jesus is saying is that if you truly love Him in spirit, you will keep His words and follow Him. And when you do this, His Spirit comes and lives within you; you gain His Spirit.

Our Commitment

When we confess with our mouth that we believe with our heart that the Lord Jesus was raised from the dead and ask Him to come into our heart to be our Lord and Savior, we have made a commitment to the Lord and to follow His Word. We take God at His Word, so He takes us at ours. Jesus said,

> But I say to you that for every idle word men may speak, they shall give account of it in the Day of Judgment. For by your words you will be justified, and by your words you will be condemned. (Matt. 12:36–37)

God makes us accountable for our words, every one of them, especially when those words are a commitment to follow Him.

Therefore, when we make a commitment to him, He expects us to follow through with that commitment. We expect God to follow through with His commitments and promises; why shouldn't He expect the same from us? God knows we will struggle with keeping this commitment, which is why He sends us a Helper. This makes it possible for when we confess Him to be our Lord and Savior, through His grace, He saves us and gives us eternal life. That is a promise, but that promise comes with expectations. When you make someone your Lord, you do His will, not as you will to do.

You're given a new life and spirit, and with that life and spirit, you're expected to follow His will and way. That is the meaning of being born again, being reborn or converted to a new way of living. God will help you with the process of being reborn, but you have to make a conscious effort to follow through with your commitment. And the first step in following through with your commitment is by reading His Word. And if you think about it, in a Jewish sense, which is Jesus telling us we have to be converted to a new way of living through His Spirit. We can now start to gain a better understanding of what our commitment is and what it means to be born again.

4

Becoming Sons of God

Just as He chose us in Him before the foundation of the world, that we should be holy and without blame before Him in love, having predestined us to adoption as sons by Jesus Christ to Himself, according to the good pleasure of His will.

—Ephesians 1:4–5

When you give your heart to God, ask Christ Jesus to become your Lord and Savior, fully submit to Him, and submerge yourself in Him and His Word, then receive and take hold of the Holy Spirit, to guide you, teach you, and change you into a new creation born of God, you become His son with an inheritance of promise and power. You gain understanding, discernment, and wisdom that will fill you with peace and joy that isn't from this world. You are filled with the power to overcome every situation you encounter, whether it is trials, tribulations, fear, worry, or pain, with pure confidence and reassurance that He who is in you is greater than he who is in this world. You become a son of the Almighty God and Father of all creation.

Faith in Christ

So let's address this a little more, the meaning of being in Christ. Saint Paul tells us,

> For you are all sons of God through faith in Christ Jesus. For as many of you as were baptized into Christ have put on Christ. (Gal. 3:26–27)

Before I go too far with this, let's take a look at "faith." What is faith, and how do we obtain it? First let's look at the meaning of faith, and then we will look at how we obtain it. The word "faith" in Greek is *pistis* (pis'-tis), meaning

1. Conviction of the truth of anything, belief; in the NT of a conviction or belief respecting man's relationship to God and divine things, generally with the included idea of trust and holy fervor born of faith and joined with it
    a) Relating to God
        1) The conviction that God exists and is the creator and ruler of all things, the provider and bestower of eternal salvation through Christ
    b) Relating to Christ
        1) A strong and welcome conviction or belief that Jesus is the Messiah, through whom we obtain eternal salvation in the kingdom of God
    c) The religious beliefs of Christians
    d) Belief with the predominate idea of trust (or confidence) whether in God or Christ, springing from faith in the same
2. Fidelity, faithfulness
    a) The character of one who can be relied on

We see here the meaning of faith is conviction of the truth of anything, being convicted, being sure of, knowing for certain, believing. Belief with the predominate idea of trust, being confident to the point of relying on it, a confident expectation. When you have faith in Christ, you trust and believe in Him to the point you rely on Him, and what He says is true with confidence and expectation.

Faith is the foundation of our relationship with God and the Lord Jesus; without faith, there can be no relationship. We must have a deep inner conviction, a confident expectation in our hearts that God is true and will do as He says. Our faith is the core of our belief in Christ. Without a confident expectation in Him, we truly can't believe in Him.

Since it is through faith in Christ Jesus that we become sons of God, let us now look at how we obtain faith. The scriptures tell us,

> Now faith is the substance of things hoped for,
> the evidence of things not seen. (Heb. 11:1)

So faith is the substance, or confident expectation, of things hoped for; and we have this confident expectation because of things not seen. Then the writer of Hebrews, after he writes this scripture, goes on to give a report of things that have happened in the past, things we haven't seen, but things that have happened, to give us this confident expectation. We didn't witness or see the things God and Christ Jesus did; we only heard of them through reading His Word. So we gain faith in Christ Jesus by reading and hearing about how God and Christ Jesus have moved in the lives of others so we may gain a confident expectation that He will move in ours.

Faith comes by hearing, hearing the Word of God. Remember the disciples asked Jesus to increase their faith, and He spoke to them. We need Jesus to speak to our hearts as well so we may have faith in Him. The Word of God tells us,

> Without faith it is impossible to please Him, for
> he who comes to God must believe that He is,

and that He is a rewarder of those who diligently seek Him. (Heb. 11:6)

And without faith and belief, it is impossible to please God and be His son.

Peter tells us,

> The genuineness of your faith, being much more precious than gold that perishes, though it is tested by fire, may be found to praise, honor, and glory at the revelation of Jesus Christ, whom having not seen you love. Though now you do not see Him, yet believing, you rejoice with joy inexpressible and full of glory, receiving the end of your faith—the salvation of your souls. (1 Pet. 1:7–9)

The genuineness or your faith is more precious than gold; it is the means to the salvation of your soul. Your faith brings praise, honor, and glory to our Lord Jesus the Christ; and this pleases Him.

Many say they have faith in God and the Lord Jesus, but do they really? Do you have faith? Do you have the confident expectation that God will reward you for diligently seeking Him? Or do you have the saving faith of confidence and trust in the Lord Jesus, that He will deliver you from whatever trouble you face, give you the strength to overcome any tragedy, and know in your heart that He will work all these things out for your own good? The confident expectation like a small child has in their parent. This is the faith one must have in God and the Lord Jesus; this is the faith that comes from one that truly believes.

James, the Lord's half brother, spells it out clearly in his letter to the twelve tribes of Israel. He says,

> My brethren, count it all joy when you fall into various trials, knowing that the testing of your faith produces patience. But let patience have its

> perfect work, that you may be complete, lacking nothing. (James 1:2–4)

You're going to face trials and tribulations in life; it's inevitable, not because God wants you to, but because this world is full of corruption and every kind of evil. What God will do though is see if one trusts in Him and has faith that He will work it all out.

Then James goes on to say,

> If any of you lacks wisdom, let him ask of God, who gives to all liberally and without reproach, and it will be given to him. But let him ask in faith, with no doubting, for he who doubts is like a wave of the sea driven and tossed by the wind. For let not that man suppose that he will receive anything from the Lord. (James 1:5–7)

If you ask something from the Lord Jesus, ask with confident expectation. If you face a trial, face it with confident expectation in the Lord, that He will help you overcome it. That is faith.

James says faith without action is dead. He said,

> What does it profit, my brethren, if someone says he has faith but does not have works? Can faith save him? If a brother or sister is naked and destitute of daily food, and one of you says to them, "Depart in peace, be warm and filled," but you do not give them the things needed for the body, what does it profit? Thus also faith by itself, if it does not have works, is dead. (James 2:14–17)

If one has faith in the Lord, then their deeds will show it. There is no faith without action. I will say that again, there is no faith without action. I'm going to be very blunt here, and if it offends you, then you may want to do some self-analysis. If you say you have faith in

Christ Jesus and your actions don't show it, then in reality you're a liar, and all you're doing is running your mouth.

James spells it out quite clearly when he says,

> Show me your faith without your works, and I will show you my faith by my works. You believe that there is one God. You do well. Even the demons believe—and tremble! (James 2:18–19)

What he is saying here is that if you truly believe and have faith in God, then your actions will show it. The demons believe in God and their actions show it; they tremble, meaning there is no way to truly believe in God and not show it.

James gives Abraham as an example of faith justified by action.

> Was not our father justified by works when he offered Isaac his son on the altar? Do you see that faith was working together with his works, and by works faith was made perfect? And the Scripture was fulfilled which says, "Abraham believed God, and it was accounted to him for righteousness." And he was called the friend of God. You see then that a man is justified by works, and not by faith only. (James 2:21–24)

As you can see, without action there is no faith, and without faith there is no salvation. You can't earn your salvation by doing good, but you show you salvation by the good you do!

The Adoption

Now that you have a clear understanding of what faith is and what it means to be baptized into Christ, let's continue with what Paul was saying in the letter to Galatia about being sons of God.

> But when the fullness of the time had come, God sent forth His Son, born of a woman, born under the law, to redeem those who were under the law, that we might receive the adoption as sons. And because you are sons, God has sent forth the Spirit of His Son into your hearts, crying out, "Abba, Father!" Therefore you are no longer a slave but a son, and if a son, then an heir of God through Christ. (Gal. 4:4–7)

Jesus came to redeem us, that we might receive the adoption as sons.

Now you may ask, "Why do we have to be adopted by God to become His children?" Aren't we His children already? Didn't He create us?" We are God's creation, and when we are in our mother's womb, God gives each of us certain talents, traits, characteristics, personalities, and everything that makes us individually different from one another. But just because God creates each and every one of us doesn't make us His children. We are direct descendants of Adam, and therefore, we are Adam's children until we are adopted by God through the Lord Jesus the Christ.

And because we are Adam's descendants, we have inherited our sinful nature from Adam because of his one act of disobedience he committed before having any children.

> Therefore, as through one man's offense judgment came to all men, resulting in condemnation, even so through one Man's righteous act the free gift came to all men, resulting in justification of life. For as by one man's disobedience many were made sinners, so also by one Man's obedience many will be made righteous. (Rom. 5:18–19)

IF WE ARE SAVED, ARE WE PROMISED HEAVEN?

Since we inherited disobedience, sin, from Adam, we have been separated from God, resulting in judgment and condemnation. As was spoken by Isaiah,

> But your iniquities have separated you from your God; and your sins have hidden His face from you, so that He will not hear. (Isa. 59:2)

Because of this separation from God, we are unable to have a relationship with Him as a Father with His children. Without the reconciliation of this separation, and the adoption to become His children, through the Lord Jesus the Christ, we face condemnation and death.

> For the wages of sin is death, but the gift of God is eternal life in Christ Jesus our Lord. (Rom. 6:23)

The apostle John puts it another way,

> But as many as received Him, to them He gave the right to become children of God, to those who believe in His name; who were born, not of blood, nor of the will of the flesh, nor of the will of man, but of God. (John 1:12–13)

There are three main things to focus on in these two verses. Two are in verse 12, and one is in verse 13. But before I go on, we must look at verse 12 in the King James Version first so we can have the true meaning of what John is telling us.

The King James Version is written like this:

> But as many as received him, to them gave he power to become the sons of God, even to them that believe on his name. (John 1:12)

And verse 13 remains the same as the NKJV. So you see the difference: if you receive Christ, you're given the power to become sons of God. Now the two words I want to focus on here are "received" and "power."

The word "received" here is *lambano*, the same word used in reference to receiving the Holy Spirit. In this verse, when John tells us "as many as received Him," i.e., Christ, he is saying we must unite and become one with Christ. We must lay hold upon, strive to obtain, take possession of, take upon one's self, give Christ access to one's self; receiving Christ is being baptized in Him, fully submerging yourself in Him, and making Him part of you.

The word "power" in Greek is *exousia* (ex-oo-see'-ah), meaning

1. Power of choice, liberty of doing as one pleases
   a) Leave or permission
2. Physical and mental power
   a) The ability or strength with which one is endued, which he either possesses or exercises
3. The power of authority (influence) and of right (privilege)
4. The power of rule or government (the power of him whose will and commands must be submitted to by others and obeyed)
   a) Universally
      1) Authority over mankind
   b) Specifically
      1) The power of judicial decisions
      2) Of authority to manage domestic affairs
   c) Metonymically
      1) A thing subject to authority or rule
      4c
      a) Jurisdiction

2) One who possesses authority
   a) A ruler, a human magistrate 4c
   b) The leading and more powerful among created beings superior to man, spiritual potentates
d) A sign of the husband's authority over his wife
   1) The veil with which propriety required a woman to cover herself
e) The sign of regal authority, a crown

This isn't just some ordinary right, like the right to freedom of speech or the right to vote. This is an anointing of power, a power of authority and strength, the anointing of becoming a prince with regal authority and control, possessing mental and physical strength over your life and circumstances. When you submerge yourself in Christ and you strive to obtain Him, take possession and lay ahold of Him, unite with Him and become as one, you are anointed with the royal power of being God's son.

Which brings me to the third point I wanted to bring to your attention about this Scripture. That is, that this power or anointing doesn't come by being born in a certain bloodline, it doesn't come by the flesh or human nature, and it doesn't come by the will of man. God gives this power to you; you're given power, anointed by the Almighty God to become His son and heir to His kingdom.

Before I go on, I want to clarify the meaning of being a Son of God. Being a Son of God is not, I repeat is not, a reference to gender but a reference to position of power. For all the women and young ladies reading this, please do not think I'm being biased in this chapter. When the Bible speaks about being a Son of God, it speaks of the position of inheritance or authority of power the son receives from the father. When a father has a son, the son inherits what the father has and is given authority over it all. But when a father has a daughter, she is given away in marriage to a son of another and inherits what that son has.

So when you, regardless of your gender, male or female, are united with Christ, you're given the position of power that the son inherits. So in other words, the term "Son of God" is about the position of power or inheritance, not about being male or female. If I were to metaphorically say children or child of God, as you may see from time to time in different translations of the Bible, the meaning loses its significance, because not all the children born from a father have the same position of authority and birthright. I'm sorry, but it is true. As I said, the daughter is given away in marriage and the son remains. That was the way it was then; inheritance was according to birthright. So in this particular scripture, in order to keep the significance of the meaning, you must not change the wording.

> Behold what manner of love the Father has bestowed on us, that we should be called children of God. (1 John 3:1)

Because of the unending love God has toward us, He has allowed us to become adopted as His children through our love for and belief in the Lord Jesus the Christ. With this adoption comes an inheritance of that as a son, and with that inheritance comes an anointing of power and Spirit. Now we are His children, God can now send us the Spirit of Christ into our hearts. You see then, when we submerge ourselves in Christ, we are reconciled to God and adopted as children, gaining a Spirit of Christ and inheriting eternal life rather than condemnation and death.

The Anointing

> The anointing which you have received from Him abides in you, and you do not need that anyone teach you; but as the same anointing teaches you concerning all things, and is true, and is not a lie, and just as it has taught you, you will abide in Him. (1 John 2:27)

When you submerge yourself in Christ and are adopted as a Son of God, you then are anointed. And this anointing in turn teaches you concerning all things; it guides your heart so you will abide in Him.

Let's look at the word "anointing" here in Greek so we have a full understanding of exactly what takes place when we submerge ourselves in Christ. The word "anointing" used in this verse in Greek is *chrisma* (khris'-mah), meaning

1. Anything smeared on, unguent, ointment, usually prepared by the Hebrews from oil and aromatic herbs.
    a) Anointing was the inaugural ceremony for priests, and sometimes also prophets, and by it they were regarded as endued with the Holy Spirit and divine gifts.
2. Is used of the gift of the Holy Spirit, as the efficient aid in getting the knowledge of the truth.

So you see here that this is a special smearing on or a pouring on of the Holy Spirit. Let's also look at the root word of *chrisma* in Greek, and that is *chrio* (khree'-o), meaning

1. To anoint
    a) Consecrating Jesus to the Messianic office, and furnishing Him with the necessary powers for its administration
    b) Enduing Christians with the gifts of the Holy Spirit

If you were to look up the root word for *chrio*, it would say probably akin to *chraomai* through the idea of contact, *chraomai* (khrä'-o-mī) meaning

1. To grant a loan, to lend
   a) The radical sense as "to furnish what is needed"
2. To receive a loan; to borrow
3. To take for one's use; to use
   a) To make use of a thing
      1) The good things of this world
      2) The opportunity to of becoming free
      3) Of a virtue or vise describing the mode of thinking or acting

    I went into depth on the meaning of anointing so you may see the full impact of what the word means and how it relates to what I said in the previous chapter about being baptized with the Holy Spirit. This anointing is what you must take hold of to use, to receive knowledge of truth, and to be set free.

    Once you become a child of God and you receive His anointing of the Holy Spirit, you must continue to abide in Christ and feed your anointing with the Word of God. This in turn allows His Spirit to grow in your heart and impact your thinking and feelings. It teaches you by convicting your heart when you sin so you can begin to become righteous and Christlike. This is the process of regeneration, being reborn as a child of God and converted to a new way of living.

    Here you have the anointing of His Spirit teaching you all things that are true and righteous. Then you have Jesus telling you,

> If you abide in My word, you are My disciples indeed. And you shall know the truth, and the truth shall make you free. (John 8:31–32)

    You have God's anointing of the Holy Spirit and His Word teaching you, guiding you, and converting you to a Christlike way of living so you can become righteous and acceptable as a Son of God.

> If you know that He is righteous, you know that everyone who practices righteousness is born of Him. (1 John 2:29)

Here we have John telling us we will know who are reborn as a Son of God by the things they practice. We know God is righteous and His Spirit is pure and true, so when we are anointed with His power and Spirit by submerging ourselves in Christ and abiding in His Word, we too will become righteous by practicing and doing things that are godly and righteous.

> Little children, let no one deceive you. He who practices righteousness is righteous, just as He is righteous. (1 John 3:7)

Let's stop and take a look at what John means by being righteous. The word John uses here for "righteous" in Greek is *dikaios* (dik'-ah-yos), meaning

1. Righteous, observing divine and human laws
    a) In a wide sense, upright, righteous, virtuous, keeping the commands of God
        1) Of those who seem to themselves to be righteous, who pride themselves to be righteous, who pride themselves in their virtues, whether real or imagined.
        2) Innocent, faultless, guiltless
            a) Having no fellowship with sin
        3) Preeminently, him whose way of thinking, feeling, and acting is wholly conformed to the will of God, and who therefore needs no rectification in the heart or life.
            a) In this sense Christ alone can be called

> 4) Approved of or acceptable of God
>   a) Acceptable to God by faith
>   b) In a narrower sense, rendering to each his due and that in a judicial sense, passing just judgment on others, whether expressed in words or shown by the manner of dealing with them.
>   1) Of god recompensing men impartially according to their deeds

So you see here that practicing righteousness is observing divine laws, keeping the commands of God, whose way of thinking, feeling, and acting is wholly conformed to the will of God. Striving to be innocent, faultless, and guiltless. Being found by others as Christ approved or acceptable of God by our outward show of obedience to the commands and will of Christ.

John tells us we know a Son of God when we see a person acting in this manner, righteous and pure. He says that those who are born of Him, a Son of God, acts like Christ acts; if you are born of Christ, you act Christlike. This is the meaning of being a Christian: Christlike. John tells us,

> And everyone who has this hope in Him [Christ] purifies himself, just as He [God] is pure. (1 John 3:3)

Then John goes even deeper into the meaning of being righteous and born of God by telling us,

> Whoever commits sin also commits lawlessness, and sin is lawlessness. And you know that He was manifested to take away our sins, and in Him there is no sin. Whoever abides in Him does

not sin. Whoever sins has neither seen Him nor
known Him. (1 John 3:4–6)

So in other words, if you are still intentionally committing sin and practicing lawlessness, then you aren't abiding in Him and therefore don't know God. And if you don't know God, how can you be His son?

Then John really drives this home when he goes on to say,

> Whoever has been born of God does not sin, for His seed remains in him; and he cannot sin, because he has been born of God. In this the children of God and the children of the devil are manifest: Whoever does not practice righteousness is not of God, nor is he who does not love his brother. For this is the message that you heard from the beginning, that we should love one another. (1 John 3:9–11)

He says that if you're not practicing righteousness and loving others, you're not born of God.

If you have been anointed as a Son of God, so that Christ and His Spirit are in you, then you will not intentionally sin. You have an anointing, a power to overcome sin and this world.

> You are of God, little children, and have overcome them, because He who is in you is greater than he who is in the world. (1 John 4:4)

> By this we know that we abide in Him, and He in us, because He has given us His Spirit. (1 John 4:13)

We know when God has anointed us with His Spirit, then we have the power to overcome sin. If you don't have this power over sin in your life, then you need to start abiding in Him and feeding your spirit so you will have the anointing of power as a Son of God.

Now don't get me wrong here, you don't just quit sinning overnight; this anointing of power isn't magic. It's a process of regeneration of the spirit. The more you feed your spirit with the Word of God and abide in Him, the stronger your spirit becomes, and the more power you gain over sin. It's the Word of God and His anointing working together in you that changes you. You can't have one without the other; it just doesn't work. That is why God, the Lord Jesus, and the Word tell us we must abide in Him. This is also why Jesus said you must be born of water and Spirit to enter the kingdom of God.

Fruit of the Spirit

When you have the anointing as a Son of God and are filled with His Spirit, you will produce fruit and bring glory to God. The fruit that you produce are Christlike qualities or characteristics given to you from His spirit. Others see these fruits by the way you act, the things you do, the way you treat others, and by the things you say.

> The fruit of the Spirit is love, joy, peace, longsuffering, kindness, goodness, faithfulness, gentleness, self-control. Against such there is no law. (Gal. 5:22–23)

If you don't have this fruit in your life, you need to start asking yourself some serious questions and make some changes. If you have given your life over to Christ, and the Spirit isn't producing these fruits in you, then you're grieving His Spirit. You're not feeding it and allowing it to grow in your heart and change you. The Spirit needs "living water" and the "bread of life" for nourishment in order to grow in you and produce fruit.

Therefore, if you are not producing the fruit of the Spirit and practicing righteousness, if you don't have the power of being God's

IF WE ARE SAVED, ARE WE PROMISED HEAVEN?

son in you, then you need to start asking yourself if you are truly reborn. You need to take a good look at what's in your heart. Do you truly believe in your heart and have faith in Christ? Or are you just professing a belief and living life however you want?

Being reborn and becoming a Son of God is a process; it's not instantaneous by saying this magic prayer as many believe. Jesus continuously tells us not to be deceived. And John also said,

> Little children, let no one deceive you. He who practices righteousness is righteous, just as He is righteous. (1 John 3:7)

And just before that,

> Whoever abides in Him does not sin. Whoever sins has neither seen Him nor known Him. (1 John 3:6)

In other words, if you're not trying to walk in a Christlike manner and be righteous, than you're not abiding in Christ, and you don't know Him.

Saint Paul puts it another way in his letter to the Romans.

> And even as they did not like to retain God in their knowledge, God gave them over to a debased mind, to do those things which are not fitting; being filled with all unrighteousness, sexual immorality, wickedness, covetousness, maliciousness; full of envy, murder, strife, deceit, evil-mindedness; they are whisperers, backbiters, haters, inventors of evil things, disobedient to parents, undiscerning, untrustworthy, unloving, unforgiving, unmerciful; who, knowing the righteous judgment of God, that those who practice such things are deserving of death, not only do

the same but also approve of those who practice them. (Rom. 1:28–32)

Paul tells us that those who don't like to retain God in their knowledge, those who don't like to read God's Word and learn from Him, are given over to a debased mind and practice such things that are deserving of death.

Let's take a moment here and look at "debased" and what it means. Now if you look up debased in the dictionary, you will find that it means the following:

1. To reduce in quality or value; adulterate
2. To lower in rank, dignity, or significance

And now, let's take a look at the word "debased" in Greek and see what it means. The word in Greek is *adokimos* (ä-do'-kē-mos), meaning

1. Not standing the test, not approved
    a) Properly used of metals and coins
2. That which does not prove itself such as it ought
    a) In a moral sense
    b) Unfit for, unproved, spurious, reprobate

What is Paul saying here, that God will allow those who don't want to fill their mind with the knowledge of His Word to remain unfit or unapproved? Without the knowledge of God, a person's mind is reduced in quality or value; it does not prove itself such as it ought, being filled with everything that is unrighteous and unpleasing to God. And Paul tells us that God will allow you to live in your misery and die because you don't want to take the time to retain Him in your knowledge and truly know Him.

IF WE ARE SAVED, ARE WE PROMISED HEAVEN?

Now ask yourself, do you know God? Is your heart for Him, and do your actions show it, or do you just profess to know Him? The Word of God says,

> To the pure all things are pure, but to those who are defiled and unbelieving nothing is pure; but even their mind and conscience are defiled. They profess to know God, but in works they deny Him, being abominable, disobedient, and disqualified for every good work. (Titus 1:15–16)

When you know God, His Spirit changes your heart and gives you a new conscience, which in turn changes the way you think, giving you a new mind. And this in turn changes the way you act and the things you do, producing in you good works. This is the process of regeneration, being reborn to a new creation in Christ.

It saddens me really to think of all the people who say they are "Christians" and don't know God. They're too busy living their lives and don't have time to get to know Him. They believe they know God because they go to church once a week, maybe tithe on a regular basis; some may even hang around after the sermon and socialize or fellowship with other Christians, and some of these people even serve or volunteer at their church on a regular basis and never truly know God. All these things are important and great to do, but they are not enough to please God. And if you do them, I pray you are doing them for God and not your own glory.

Serving and having fellowship with the body of Christ are a very important part of being a Christian, but these things don't change you. They do help you in the process of changing, which is why they are important. The idea is to be around and fellowship with the body of Christ in order to exhort one another and to guide and teach each other. But if the body of Christ doesn't know God, then these things are often just surface changes and many times are only done to make us either look good or feel good. The true change has to come from within by knowing the Word of God and His Spirit.

I only say this because I was just like that at one time. I was one of those "Christians" at one time. I had significantly seen God move in my life. I had experienced things that I knew in my heart that could have come only from God. Even today, as I look back and ponder on those experiences, I know God was getting my attention. After that, I went to church every weekend, never missed a Sunday. I joined a small group on Fridays and started serving or volunteering on Sundays. As a matter of fact, I served all three services at my church every Sunday and was at the church from early morning until the afternoon. I even made my son go and serve too. I did this for several years, even joined other small groups during that period, sometimes two to three groups a week. My heart was for God. I made promises to Him and was dedicated to serving Him for what He had done for me.

But all that time I never really knew Him, and I never really changed either. I thought I did. I was going through all the motions and doing all the things I thought I was supposed to do. By going to church, serving, joining small groups, I was being an active member in the body of Christ. I was born again, and I was doing what "Christians" do. And by doing these things, I thought I knew God.

I mean, really, I was going to small group Bible studies, even a couple of twelve-step Bible studies too. I thought I was studying His Word on a regular basis. But I really wasn't. I was studying books that were about His Word. They had scriptures in them; they helped you interpret what the scriptures mean and apply them to your life. But in reality, they were books written by pastors, not God. I'm not saying those little Bible study booklets, study guides, commentaries, and other books written by pastors and church leaders are bad. By no means, those books are great tools and help us significantly, but they don't have the same impact as reading the Bible itself and spending time getting to know God personally. Taking the time to read the Bible directly and allowing it to speak directly to your heart is where the true power of change comes from.

Many may say the Bible was written by men too; they will even say that most of the New Testament was written by Paul, who didn't even walk with Christ. He may not have walked with Christ personally in the flesh during His ministry, but he definitely walked with Christ spiritually. Besides, the Holy Spirit through man wrote all the scriptures.

> And so we have the prophetic word confirmed, which you do well to heed as a light that shines in a dark place, until the day dawns and the morning star rises in your hearts; knowing this first, that no prophecy of Scriptures is of any private interpretation, for prophecy never came by the will of man, but holy men of God spoke as they were moved by the Holy Spirit. (2 Pet. 1:19–21)

So you see, the Word of God came through holy men of God by the Holy Spirit. The scriptures come from the Holy Spirit through man, and they have the power of God in them. You may say these pastors and other men are holy men too, and they have the Holy Spirit. And this may very well be true, and they were more than likely to be impelled by the Spirit to write their books to help others learn and interpret the Word of God. But always keep in mind that their words aren't considered Scripture; their words are fallible and haven't been proven by the test of time.

The Word of God has lasted thousands of years and has never been proven wrong; that all in itself is power. It has withstood the criticism and testing of thousands and thousands of scholars, professors, and scientists. All these are looking to prove one thing wrong in the Bible, in order to discredit the Word of God. Man does this because if he can discredit the Word of God, then he could justify his selfish and sinful nature and not be held accountable for his actions. But the Word of God is alive and thriving, it has the power to change the lives of mankind, and nothing else can stand up to this power. It is through this power that we become sons of God.

5

Salvation and Heaven

You have also given me the shield of Your salvation;
Your right hand has held me up, Your gentleness has made me great.

—Psalms 18:35

We in our society today want as much as we can get for as little as possible; we want everything for free. With technology being as advanced as it is, and advancing more and more at a breathtaking rate, mankind is becoming more accustomed to applying less effort to accomplish things each day. And as our technology advances, things become easier and easier to do: building, traveling, working, reading, writing, cleaning, communication, etc. You name it; the list goes on and on. If it applies effort, man has found a way to do it easier.

Tools, machinery, and heavy equipment have made building easier; homes, commercial buildings, luxury resorts, apartment complexes, and high-rises go up in lightning speed. Man can dig a hole big enough for a train, sit down in air-conditioning, listen to the radio while eating sunflower seeds, and never break a sweat. With computers and the World Wide Web, we can work from anywhere—our homes, coffee shops, our vehicles, our bathrooms, and our bedrooms all have become our office. Some people don't even have to get out of bed to go to work. We have programs on our computers that correct and edit as we type. Many of us don't even use a pen and paper to write anymore unless we sign our name on a document printed from a printer. My older children do their homework on the computer and turn it in online now; sometimes they even do it on their phones while on the bus coming home from school. Traveling is just as easy; we sit comfortably in our cars or on a plane as we travel from one destination to another.

There is nothing wrong with these advancements, by no means at all; they are awesome and great. Technology is supposed to make things quicker and easier for us. The problem is mankind wants "going to heaven" to be just as easy. People want to just say a magic prayer, simply ask for the forgiveness of their sins, and believe that they are going to heaven. They want to live their lives the same way they always have and believe that it is all right, because at the end of the day, they need only to ask to be forgiven. People want to have their cake and eat it too, especially when it comes to going to heaven. They want a free ride to paradise, paid for by Christ.

A Free Ride from Christ

This may be the most controversial subject of all time concerning the gospel; do we work for our salvation and place in heaven, or is it a free gift from God? You hear it preached all the time, "You can't earn your salvation. It's not by works but by grace you are saved." And this is true, very true; your salvation is by the grace of God. People couldn't earn their salvation. They are full of corruption and sin, and their hearts are hard and full of deceit. That is why God had to send His Son, Jesus the Christ, to do it for us. That was grace; it was by the grace of God that He made a way for us, and that way is through Jesus. But don't be deceived. Our way for salvation was a free gift from God, but putting our faith and trust in Christ Jesus to get to heaven isn't free.

Heaven is a reward for our belief and faith in Christ Jesus, and it takes a conscious effort on our part to get there. If you think you can continue living your life however you want and just ask to be forgiven on a daily basis and that you're going to heaven, think again. The thing is many people believe this; they believe they can just profess a belief in Jesus and they are going to heaven. That's not what the Lord Jesus tells us in the Bible though, and many people don't know this because they don't read their Bibles. These people are going to be very surprised on that last day, the day of judgment, when the Lord tells them,

> I never knew you, depart from Me, you who practice lawlessness! (Matt. 7:23)

You may think I'm crazy or I don't know what I'm talking about when I tell you heaven is a reward, and we must earn it. That's right, I said earn it; we must work for our place in heaven. Oh, I know what you're saying right now, "It's not by works; it's by grace" or "It's not by what we do; it's by what Jesus did on the cross," and so on. I can picture it right now: many who are reading this are grabbing their Bibles to find the scriptures to prove me wrong, and that's great. The meaning of this book is to get you to read your Bible and search the scriptures. I tell you what, let me help you out. I will list all these scriptures for you so we can go over them.

> Now to him who works, the wages are not counted as grace but as debt. (Rom. 4:4)

> But to him who does not work but believes on Him who justifies the ungodly, his faith is accounted for righteousness. (Rom. 4:5)

> For the children not yet being born, nor having done any good or evil, that the purpose of God according to election might stand, not of works but of Him who calls. (Rom. 9:11)

And if by grace, then [it is] no longer of works; otherwise grace is no longer grace. But if [it is] of works, it is no longer grace; otherwise work is no longer work. (Rom. 11:6)

Knowing that a man is not justified by the works of the law but by faith in Jesus Christ, even we have believed in Christ Jesus, that we might be justified by faith in Christ and not by the works of the law; for by the works of the law no flesh shall be justified. (Gal. 2:16)

This only I want to learn from you: Did you receive the Spirit by the works of the law, or by the hearing of faith? (Gal. 3:2)

Therefore He who supplies the Spirit to you and works miracles among you, [does He do it] by the works of the law, or by the hearing of faith? (Gal. 3:5)

For by grace you have been saved through faith, and that not of yourselves; it is the gift of God, not of works, lest anyone should boast. (Eph. 2:8–9)

Who has saved us and called [us] with a holy calling, not according to our works, but according to His own purpose and grace which was given to us in Christ Jesus before time began. (2 Tim. 1:9)

Not by works of righteousness which we have done, but according to His mercy He saved us, through the washing of regeneration and renewing of the Holy Spirit. (Titus 3:9)

Well, those are all the scriptures, or most of them anyway, that you hear preached in church about how you can't earn your salvation or righteousness by what you do. And that's true, it's right there, and the Word of God says it, and I'm not denying it one bit. You can't earn your salvation, and there is nothing you can do to get in right standing with God. You only obtain that through faith and belief in His Son, Jesus the Christ. But you will notice that nowhere in these scriptures does it mention anything about heaven; they only speak of our salvation and righteousness.

The Sugarcoated Version

Before I get into the difference between salvation and heaven, I want to explain why many people believe that because they are saved they are going to heaven. The main reason is that they don't read their Bibles, and before they do, they should pray for wisdom and understanding concerning the Word of God. They would rather do what's easy: by going to church once a week for an hour and listening to what the pastor tells them. The thing is, the pastor only has about forty minutes to deliver the sermon; and oftentimes, the message is light. This isn't always the case, but unfortunately for most churches, it is.

Many churches want to keep the seats full; so they have a great worship team with a big stage, lots of lights, and huge TVs with cool video productions. They have a charismatic pastor and have all kinds of famous people come and talk about their faith; they put on a nice show for the people. And this is fine; if they are bringing people to Christ, more power to them. But oftentimes, their message is light, and they are only telling the people the parts of the Bible that the people want to hear. So the seats would remain full, they give the sugarcoated version of the gospel. They're afraid if they preached the whole truth, people won't come to their church, and their church won't prosper.

This is why the church is so weak today, because they don't have the faith and trust in God to preach the whole truth of the gospel. Jesus predicted this when He said,

> Take heed that no one deceives you. For many will come in My name, saying, "I am the Christ," and will deceive many. (Matt. 24:4–5)

What Jesus is saying here is that many will come in the name of the Lord, representing Him, and will deceive many. Many think that because it says, "I am the Christ," in this scripture, it means someone will come claiming to be the Christ or something of that sort. That isn't what it means. "I am the Christ" means the body of Christ, and the body of Christ is the church. Many will come in His name; the church will come and deceive many. Christ warns us not to be deceived many times; this is why He says to learn from Him.

Look what Paul writes in his second letter to Timothy:

> Preach the word! Be ready in season and out of season. Convince, rebuke, exhort, with all longsuffering and teaching. For the time will come when they will not endure sound doctrine, but according to their own desires, because they have itching ears, they will heap up for themselves teachers; and they will turn their ears away from the truth, and be turned aside to fables. (2 Tim. 4:2–4)

Paul said to preach the Word and be ready at all times, in and out of season. To convince, rebuke, and exhort with all longsuffering and teaching, meaning preach and teach the Word in truth no matter what you may endure.

Paul said that there would come a time when people wouldn't endure sound doctrine because of their own desires, because the people would have itching ears. The word here for "itching" in Greek is *knetho* (knay'-tho), meaning

1. To scratch, tickle, make to itch
2. To itch
3. Desirous of hearing something pleasant

So what Paul was saying was that a time would come that people wouldn't want to hear the truth; they would want to hear things that are pleasant to their ears. So they would heap up for themselves teachers who would do just as they wanted; they would follow and listen to the pastors who make them feel good and tell them things they like to hear. Much like it is today—"Come see the show and say this magic prayer. Now you're saved, and you're going to heaven. It's free, and you don't have to do a thing. Just ask to be forgiven and say you believe." Does this sound familiar? I hear it preached all the time, and it makes me sad. Although there is some truth in what is being preached, I'm not saying the church is lying to you; it's just the sugarcoated version of the truth because that's what people want to hear.

This is why many believe that salvation and heaven are one and the same, because many churches aren't teaching the whole truth. I'm not saying there aren't any churches that teach the whole truth of the Word, because there are several really good churches that do. The only problem is that there are more churches that preach the sugarcoated version of God's Word than there are churches that teach the whole truth.

And like I said, this is why the church or body of Christ is weak today. It is growing in numbers and growing larger every day, but it is weak and doesn't possess the power of God, as it should. Why do you think we don't see the miraculous signs and healings that were witnessed in the first-century church in our church today? God hasn't changed; He remains the same today as He did back then. So we should see the same power of God displayed in our church today, as we read about in the book of Acts.

The body of Christ, the church, is supposed to be anointed with the power of the Holy Spirit. Christians are sons of God and possess the power of the Son, a power greater than this world. Jesus said,

> Most assuredly, I say to you, he who believes in Me, the works that I do he will do also; and greater works than these he will do, because I go to My Father. (John 14:12)

The body of Christ should be doing the same works as the Christ Jesus, even greater, because He has given us His power so we may bring glory to the Father. And the only requirement for this power is to believe in Him.

We don't see this power because the gospel being preached is watered down and sugarcoated. The church is preaching that it is okay not to be okay. They don't want to tell you that you're not okay and your life is all messed up because you're being disobedient to God and not doing as He commands. The church doesn't tell you that if you don't repent and change the way you are living, you are going to die and go to hell. Instead, they tell you it's okay to be all messed up because you were born a sinner, and there's nothing you can do about that but accept Christ into your heart to be your Lord and Savior, that He already did the work for you. So people believe they don't have to do anything and that there is nothing they can do to change themselves, so they sit around waiting for God to do it for them.

The truth is, it's not okay to be messed up, broken, sick, and lacking abundance. That Christ made a way for you, so start following Him and do as He tells you. It's not okay to be sick and diseased, that you possess the healing power of the Christ Jesus, and you need only to believe in it. That it's not okay to be broke and in debt, that if you follow the Lord's commands, He will open the windows of heaven and bless you with abundance. The body of Christ can't truly believe in Christ Jesus and the power it has been given, because it doesn't know the true gospel and Word of God. When the Word of

God says to obey the gospel, and the gospel tells you to follow the Lord Jesus and do as He commands, then that's what you need to do!

Following the Christ Jesus should be easy, but now it will take work and a conscious effort to do because of the way we have been raised and taught for generations now. The churches have been teaching and preaching a sugarcoated version of the gospel, feeding our flesh and egos to make us feel good so we will come to their church, to the point that now it will take some effort to change and truly follow what the Christ commands.

And it's not only our churches either; it's our society as a whole that has made it difficult to follow the Christ Jesus. We have taken God out of our schools when (here in the United States) the very concept of building schools was to teach our children how to read and write so they could read the Word of God and not be deceived by Satan. The Old Deluder Act of 1647 was passed so that when a township grew to fifty households, someone was to be appointed to teach the children to read and write so they may learn the scriptures. And when a township reached one hundred households, a school was to be built. Imagine that, our schools were developed to teach our children to read and write so they may learn the scriptures, and now it is against the law to teach about God and the Christ Jesus in them.

It is because of these reasons that it will be difficult and take some work to follow the Christ Jesus. Following Jesus will go against everything we have been taught for generations. And as long as our churches just keep preaching the sugarcoated version of the gospel, it's not going to get any easier. Our churches need to quit worrying about filling the seats and start preaching and teaching the truth. This makes you see why Jesus said,

> For many are called, but few chosen. (Matt. 20:16)

IF WE ARE SAVED, ARE WE PROMISED HEAVEN?

Salvation

Now let's go over salvation and what it means to have it. First, we will look at the meaning of salvation as it is stated in Romans 10:10, the very scripture our confession is based from:

> For with the heart one believes unto righteousness, and with the mouth confession is made unto salvation.

Here the word for "salvation" in Greek is *soteria* (so-tay-ree'-ah), meaning

1. Deliverance, preservation, safety, salvation
   a) Deliverance from the molestation of enemies
   b) In an ethical sense, that which concludes to the souls safety or salvation
      1) Of Messianic salvation
2. Salvation as the present possession of all true Christians
3. Future salvation, the sum of benefits and blessings, which the Christians, redeemed from all earthly ills, will enjoy after the visible return of Christ from heaven in the consummated and eternal kingdom of God. (Strong's)

Note: Scripture describes a fourfold salvation: saved from the penalty, power, presence, and most importantly the pleasure of sin. (A. W. Pink, *A Fourfold Salvation*)

Salvation is deliverance, preservation, and safety from the molestation of our enemies, as a present possession, and in the future eternal kingdom of God. An enemy can be anything harmful, prejudicial, or belonging to a hostile power. Our enemies are and can be sin, fear, worry, stress, sickness, disease, addiction, contempt, envy, hatred, jealousy, idolatry, contentions, and every evil work known to man.

> And the Lord will deliver me from every evil work and preserve me for His heavenly kingdom. To Him be glory forever and ever. Amen! (2 Tim. 4:18)

A person who is saved experiences salvation here and now; they experience the peace that comes from the deliverance of sin, fear, and worry. Salvation isn't just something a believer experiences after death in eternal life; it's something they experience now in this life that preserves them for eternal life.

Now let's look at the word "preserve" in this last verse, and you will see how it pertains to salvation. "Preserve" in Greek is *sozo* (sō'-zō), meaning

1. To save, keep safe and sound, to rescue from danger or destruction
    a) One (from injury or peril)
        1) To save a suffering one (from perishing), i.e. one suffering from disease, to make well, heal, restore to health
        2) To preserve one who is in danger of destruction, to save or rescue
    b) To save in the technical biblical sense
        1) Negatively
            a) To deliver from the penalties of the Messianic judgment
            b) To save from the evils which obstruct the reception of the Messianic deliverance

> c) To save from the punitive wrath of God at the judgment of the last day

> Salvation begins in this life, in deliverance from error and corrupt notions, in moral purity, in pardon of sin, and in the blessed peace of a soul reconciled to God. (Thayer's)

Salvation is deliverance, preservation, healing, safety, and restoration from sin, sickness, disease, stress, fear, worry, etc. In essence, if you truly believe in Christ Jesus and are saved, then you should be experiencing the power of God's salvation in your life today. The church, the body of Christ, should be experiencing the power of God's salvation today!

Remember what Jesus said in John 3:16–17:

> For God so loved the world that He gave His only begotten Son, that whoever believes in Him should not perish but have everlasting life. For God did not send His Son into the world to condemn the world, but that the world through Him might be saved [sozo].

So you see here that it is through Christ Jesus that we are kept safe and sound from suffering, danger, and destruction. When a follower of Christ Jesus submerges himself or herself in Him, follows His commands, and lives righteously and holy, then God puts a hedge around them and protects and preserves them from the evils of this world. Jesus promises us everlasting life and saves us from condemnation through our belief in Him. This is our salvation, that we should be preserved and have eternal life.

Believing in Christ

An important thing to know here is what the Lord means when He says "that whoever believes in Him." The word "believes" in Greek is *pisteuo* (pist-yoo'-o), meaning

1. To think to be true, to be persuaded of, to credit, place confidence in
    a) Of the thing believed
        1) To credit, have confidence
    b) In moral or religious reference
        1) Used in the NT of the conviction and trust to which a man is impelled by a certain inner and higher prerogative and law of soul
        2) To trust in Jesus or God as able to aid either in obtaining or in doing something: saving faith
            a) To place reliance on
                1) Mere acknowledgment of some fact or event: intellectual faith
2. To entrust a thing to one, i.e. his fidelity
    a) To be entrusted with a thing
    b) To commit one's self trustfully to
3. A conviction, full of joyful trust, that Jesus is the Messiah—the divinely appointed author of eternal salvation in the kingdom of God, conjoined with obedience to Christ
    a) To have a faith directed unto, believing or in faith to give one's self up to Jesus

Thus, the meaning of "believing in Christ" is being persuaded of and placing your confidence in Him to the point of being impelled by a certain inner and higher prerogative and law of soul to trust that He is able to aid you in everything—entrusting yourself to Him. This belief isn't just merely saying some words; it's a deep inner conviction of your mind and soul that He is there to aid you in every way, to the point that you surrender and entrust yourself in obedience to Him.

When you come to the point of this deep inner conviction of belief and trust in the living Son of God, Jesus the Christ our Lord, He gives you the gift of the eternal kingdom of God, everlasting life. What does that mean, everlasting life? Does the Lord Jesus say that if we believe in Him He is going to give us heaven? No, He clearly says everlasting life, life that never ends. Let's look at the word "everlasting" in Greek; it is *aionios* (ahee-o'-nee-os), meaning

1. Without beginning and end, that which always has been and always will be
2. Without beginning
    a) Whose subject-matter is eternal, i.e. the saving purpose of God adopted from eternity
3. Without end, never to cease, everlasting

Before I go on, let's look at the word "life" too. The word "life" is *zoe* (zō-ā'), meaning

1. Life
    a) The state of one who is possessed of vitality or is animate
    b) Every living soul
        1) Spoken of earthly life
        2) A promise looking to the present and the future life
2. Life
    a) Of the absolute fullness of life, both essential and ethical, which belongs to God, and through him both to the hypostatic "logos" put on human nature
    b) Life real and genuine, a life active and vigorous, devoted to God, blessed, in

> the portion even in this world of those who put their trust in Christ, but after the resurrection to be consummated by new accessions (among them a more perfect body), and to last for ever.

So you see here, everlasting life is without beginning or end; it's here and now and forevermore. It's life that is real and genuine, active and vigorous, blessed with absolute fullness. Jesus says if you believe in Him, truly *pisteuo* in Him, He will give you life (*zoe*) without end—a life (*zoe*) never to cease, now and forever. This is the promise He gives us: that when we entrust ourselves to Him, fully and deeply to the very inch of our soul, He will give us a life of the absolute fullness and blessed. We are meant to experience that life now and with Him in heaven, but that depends on if you truly believe in Him and how you act on that belief.

Christ as Our Lord

Before we start talking about heaven, let's go into more depth about what it means to believe in Christ Jesus and what it means to make Him Lord of our life. I want to clarify even more what it means to make Jesus our Lord, because when we truly believe and entrust our very soul to Him, when we have that deep conviction of trust in Him, we then will submerge ourselves in Him and love Him. We will want to please Him with everything that we are, by doing the very things He desires, doing as He commands, which in turn is the will of the Father. I say this because making Jesus our Lord is part of our confession, the very confession that is made unto salvation.

The Word of God says,

> If you confess with your mouth the Lord Jesus and believe [*pisteuo*] in your heart that God has raised Him from the dead, you will be saved. (Rom. 10:9)

IF WE ARE SAVED, ARE WE PROMISED HEAVEN?

Okay, we are going to break this down too; I want you to know what kind of confession you are making here and the impact of it. The word "confess" here in Greek is *homologeo* (hom-ol-og-eh'-o), meaning

1. To say the same thing as another, i.e. to agree with, assent
2. To concede
   a) Not to refuse, to promise
   b) Not to deny
      1) To confess
      2) Declare
      3) To confess, i.e. to admit or declare one's self guilty of what one is accused of
3. To profess
   a) To declare openly, speak out freely
      1) To declare fully, implying the yielding or change of one's conviction
      2) That which one is convinced and which one holds to be true
   b) To profess one's self the worshipper of one
4. To praise, celebrate

You see here your confession is to concede, not to refuse, to promise with our mouth that Christ Jesus is your Lord. You are making a declaration and a promise to the Lord Jesus that He is your Lord; and thus, through your belief or *pisteuo* that God raised Him up from the dead, He saves you. Are you getting how this works? That you are making a confession or *homologeo*, a full and unyielding declaration of promise with your mouth to Jesus as your Lord, and that you *pisteuo* in your heart that He is the Christ and was raised from the dead by God, and through this, He saves and preserves you from condemnation, now and for eternity.

We must also look at the word "Lord" in Greek and what it means. The word "Lord" in Greek is *Kurios* (koo'-ree-os), meaning

1. He to whom a person or thing belongs, about which he has power of deciding; master, lord
    a) The possessor and disposer of a thing
        1) The owner; one who has control of the person, the master
        2) In the state: the sovereign, prince, chief, the Roman emperor
    b) Is a title of honor expressive of respect and reverence, with which servants greet their master
    c) This title is given to: God, the Messiah

As we can see here, the meaning of "Lord" is very significant. It means that when we make a declaration or promise to Him, we belong to Him, that He has deciding power over us. We make Him our Master, the Lord over our life with honor expressive of respect and reverence. That means we do as He says. We follow His will; He is our owner and in control of our lives, in which we follow His way of living, not our own.

I want you to have a clear understanding of what it means to confess Jesus as our Lord, what it means to truly believe in your heart making Him your Savior, so that you will have a clear understanding of what salvation is. A person needs to know the meaning of making Jesus their Lord because it makes a difference in their salvation as well as where they spend eternity. Like I said before, God takes us at our word; He holds us accountable for the words we confess, every one of them. If we make a confession or a declaration (promise) to Him or to the world (baptism), we are held accountable for what we say, and we are to uphold our commitment.

Because when we make that confession, God and the Lord Jesus gives us a Helper, the Holy Spirit, to walk with and within us as we become reborn to a new way of life. So as you may start to realize and understand, our confession is a commitment to Jesus, in which we become reborn to a new way of living; and it takes a conscious effort on our part to fulfill this commitment by submerging ourselves in Christ. And God made this obtainable for us through His Son the Christ Jesus because of His unyielding mercy and grace.

Heaven and the Way

Before I get too far with this, let's now clarify what heaven is or what we consider heaven to be. Heaven is spending eternity in the presence of the Lord, entering into His rest. In Revelations 21:1–4, John writes,

> Now I saw a new heaven and a new earth, for the first heaven and the first earth had passed away. Also there was no more sea. Then I, John, saw the holy city, New Jerusalem, coming down out of heaven from God, prepared as a bride adorned for her husband. And I heard a loud voice from heaven saying, "Behold, the tabernacle of God is with men, and He will dwell with them, and they shall be His people. God Himself will be with them and be their God. And God will wipe away every tear from their eyes; there shall be no more death, nor sorrow, nor crying. There will be no more pain, for the former things have passed away." (Rev. 21:1–4)

It says the new tabernacle of God or holy place is with men, and He shall dwell with them. The new heaven will be with God, and He will be with His people. We will live in the presence of the Lord Jesus and God the Father.

So let's look at the word "heaven" here. In Greek, it's *ouranos* (oo-ran-os'), meaning

1. The vaulted expanse of the sky with all things visible in it
   a) The universe, the world
      1) According to the primitive Hebrew manner of speaking, inasmuch as they had neither the conception nor the name of "the universe"
   b) The aerial heavens or sky, the region where the clouds and the tempests gather, and where thunder and lightning are produced
   c) The sidereal or starry heavens
2. The region above the sidereal heavens, the seat of order of things eternal and consummately perfect where God dwells and other heavenly beings
   a) Is appointed as the future abode of those who, raised from the dead and clothed with superior bodies, shall become partakers of the heavenly kingdom, and enjoy the reward of proved virtue.

As we can see here, heaven is where God and other heavenly beings dwell. And where God is, Jesus is also, since He is at His right hand. And to get into the presence of God, we must go through the Lord Jesus the Christ. For the Lord Jesus said,

> I am the way, the truth, and the life. No one comes to the Father except through Me. (John 14:6)

Then again Jesus said,

> I am the door. If anyone enters by Me, he will be saved, and will go in and out and find pasture. (John 10:9)

What Jesus is saying here is when we enter through Him into the presence of God, or heaven, we shall find pasture and have rest for our souls.

6

Entering Heaven

> How awesome is this place!
> This is none other than the house of God,
> And this is the gate of heaven!
>
> —Genesis 28:17

Now we know about heaven, the meaning of it and how to get there. Let's look at who will be allowed to enter it. Let's see if God's Word tells us that everyone who is saved is going to go to heaven. I believe we will find the answer in one of the most profound statements the Lord Jesus makes in His Sermon on the Mount.

> Not everyone who says to Me, "Lord, Lord," shall enter the kingdom of heaven, but he who does the will of My Father in heaven. (Matt. 7:21)

It's very clear here what Jesus says about entering the kingdom of heaven. He said not everyone who calls Him Lord shall enter, but only those who do the will of the Father.

IF WE ARE SAVED, ARE WE PROMISED HEAVEN?

How profound is this that Jesus would tell us not everyone who calls Him Lord shall enter this heavenly kingdom but those who do the will of God? Does that sound like you can just profess Him as Lord and you're good to go, just say "Jesus is my Lord" and you're going to heaven? He said those who do the will of the Father shall enter the kingdom of heaven. So you can see here that you can profess Him as Lord, but unless you do His will, you're not going to make the cut to get into heaven. Jesus is very clear and precise on what He is saying here, that there is a difference between professing and believing, saying something and doing what you say.

Jesus said,

> But why do you call Me "Lord, Lord," and not
> do the things which I say? (Luke 6:46)

He says you call Him Lord, but you don't do as He says; or in other words, you say it, but you don't mean it. Much like it is today, people call themselves Christians, but their actions are from that of a true believer. The Pharisees and religious leaders were acting the same way with God, and Jesus brought it to their attention and called them, "Hypocrites!" Jesus said,

> These people draw near to Me with their mouth,
> and honor Me with their lips, but their heart is
> far from Me. (Matt. 15:8)

Many so-called Christians are the same way today; not much has changed from then until now. They talk about how much they love God yet never read His Word. And many people say that Jesus is their Lord and Savior and call themselves Christians but know very little about what Christ teaches. They say they love God and the Lord Jesus when the truth is they really love themselves and use the grace of God for their own selfish gain and glory. Just like the Pharisees and religious leaders said they loved God but used the law for their own selfish gain and glory.

Gathering or Scattering

When you call yourself a Christian and don't make changes in your actions and the way you think, and you just continue to live the same life you always have, people see this and are driven away from the body of Christ. They say, "Those Christians are just a bunch of hypocrites," and they want nothing to do with the church. This is what Jesus meant when He said,

> He who is not with Me is against Me, and he who does not gather with Me scatters abroad. (Matt. 12:30)

Let me explain this in more detail before we go on. Jesus said, "If you're not with Him you are against Him." The word "with" in Greek is *meta* (met-ah'), meaning

1. With, after, behind.

What this means is if you're not living a life with Him, following after His ways, behind Him in what He says, you are against Him. Jesus is saying that if you're not letting His light shine through you in your actions and deeds, you're then working against Him. You are claiming to be like Him when you call yourself a Christian, but your actions and life don't portray Him. Then He goes on to say, "If you're not gathering with Him, you're scattering." The word "gather" in Greek is *sunago* (soon-ag'-o), meaning

1. To gather together, to gather
    a) To draw together, collect
        1) Of fishes
        2) Of a net in which they are caught
2. To bring together, assemble, collect
    a) To join together, join in one (those previously separated)
    b) To gather together by convoking

c) To be gathered, i.e. come together, gather, meet
3. To lead with one's self
   a) Into one's home, i.e. to receive hospitably, to entertain

Now if your actions and deeds aren't portraying Christ, if people aren't seeing a change in the way you live and act, are you really drawing them into the body of Christ? Are you strengthening their faith that Christ has the power to change lives? Or are people saying, "Look at him. He says he believes in Christ, but he is no different now than he was before. Still the same old Joe except now he goes to church and thinks he is better than everyone else"? This is the very thing that drives or scatters people from the church. And if this is the case, what do you think Jesus is going to say to you that day when you kneel before Him? You think He is going to say, "Well done, good and faithful servant. You have been faithful over a few things. I will make you ruler over many things. Enter into the joy of your Lord" (Matt. 25:23), and then you're going to spend eternity with Him in heaven?

Conscious Effort

We are not perfect, and we have to live in this world. The Lord understands this, and that is why we live by grace. But we have to make a conscious effort to change the things we do and follow His ways. Paul tells us,

> But you, O man of God, flee these things and pursue righteousness, godliness, faith, love, patience, gentleness. Fight the good fight of faith, lay hold on eternal life, to which you were also called and have confessed the good confession in the presence of many witnesses. (1 Tim. 6:11–12)

What does Paul tell us to do? He says to fight the good fight of faith and lay hold on eternal life. That means to fight to keep your faith against what this entire world teaches you and lay hold on, to claim eternal life, your salvation! Paul says we must pursue righteousness, godliness, faith, love, patience, and gentleness. This pursuit takes a conscious effort; even more than that, we must fight against our worldly nature for it.

> If anyone teaches otherwise and does not consent to wholesome words, even the words of our Lord Jesus Christ, and to the doctrine which accords with godliness, he is proud, knowing nothing, but is obsessed with disputes and arguments over words, from which come envy, strife, reviling, evil suspicions, useless wrangling's of men of corrupt minds and destitute of the truth, who suppose that godliness is a means of gain. From such withdraw yourself. (1 Tim. 6:3–5)

Paul says to flee from these things. This is part of the good fight, and it too takes a conscious effort on the Christians' part to fight it. Do you think fleeing and pursuing doesn't take work and that you can just sit by idling doing nothing as if it's a free gift?

The Narrow Gate

Jesus knows man, and He knows our hearts. He knew following Him would be difficult for us to do. That is why Jesus said,

> Enter by the narrow gate; for wide is the gate and broad is the way that leads to destruction, and there are many who go in by it. Because narrow is the gate and difficult is the way which leads to life, and there are few who find it. (Matt. 7:13–14)

IF WE ARE SAVED, ARE WE PROMISED HEAVEN?

Jesus said difficult is the way that leads to life. It's not easy, and it takes effort. You see it is easy to live life the way the world says to, but it's difficult to go against the world's view and to live life the way God tells us to. And because it takes effort and because people believe they don't have to work for it, few will ever find the way.

In the King James Version, Matthew 7:14 is written "straight is the gate and narrow is the way." Here the word "narrow" in Greek is *thlibo* (thlee'-bo), meaning

1. To press (as grapes), press hard upon
2. A compressed way
    a) Narrow straightened, contracted
3. Metaph. to trouble, afflict, distress

And the phrase "is the way" in Greek is *hodos* (hod-os'), meaning

1. Properly
    a) A way
        1) A travelled way, road
    b) A traveller's way, journey, travelling
2. Metaph.
    a) A course of conduct
    b) A way (i.e. manner) of thinking, feeling, deciding

So what Jesus is saying is that because you have to press hard—you have to endure trouble, affliction, and distress in your course of conduct, your way of thinking, your feelings and decisions—few ever make it through the gate that leads to life. Does this sound like a free gift to you? Does it sound like you don't have to work on changing the manner of your thinking, the way you feel, and the decisions you make, in order to be approved to enter the gate?

I say approved to enter, because Jesus clearly says,

> Strive to enter through the narrow gate, for many, I say to you, will seek to enter and will not be able.

> When once the Master of the house has risen up and shut the door, and you begin to stand outside and knock at the door, saying, "Lord, Lord, open for us," and He will answer and say to you, "I do not know you, where are you from," then you will begin to say, "We ate and drank in Your presence, and You taught in our streets." But He will say, "I tell you I do not know you, where are you from. Depart from Me, all you workers of iniquity." There will be weeping and gnashing of teeth, when you see Abraham and Isaac and Jacob and all the prophets in the kingdom of God, and yourselves thrust out. (Luke 13:24–28)

Wow, how powerful and serious is that?
And in Matthew, Jesus said,

> Not everyone who says to Me, "Lord, Lord," shall enter the kingdom of heaven, but he who does the will of My Father in heaven. Many will say to Me in that day, "Lord, Lord, have we not prophesied in Your name, cast out demons in Your name, and done many wonders in Your name?" And then I will declare to them, "I never knew you; depart from Me, you who practice lawlessness!" (Matt. 7:21–23)

Again, Jesus tells those who call upon His name, the ones who call Him Lord, the "believers" who continue to practice lawlessness with no regard for His commands, to depart from Him that He never knew you.

There are several things I want to bring to your attention concerning these passages. If you notice, Jesus says, "Strive to enter through the narrow gate." The word "strive" in Greek is *agonizomai* (ag-o-nid'-zom-ahee), meaning

1. To enter a contest: contend in the gymnastic games
2. To contend with adversaries, fight
3. Metaph. to contend, struggle, with difficulties and dangers
4. To endeavor with strenuous zeal, strive: to obtain something

Jesus is telling us we have to contend, struggle, and fight with difficulties and adversaries, to endeavor with strenuous zeal to obtain something. That something you are to strive to obtain is to follow Him and do the will of His Father in heaven. You are to endeavor with strenuous zeal to do as He commands, against what the world tells you, what your ego tells you, what your flesh tells you, and what the adversary throws at you. It's not always going to be easy, and truthfully, it's not very hard either because Jesus already won the battle for us. We just need to make a conscious effort on our part to learn from Him, and what we learn from Him, we put into practice. Changing the way we think and the things we do takes some work on our part; it doesn't come naturally or magically. Again, we must fight the good fight of faith.

Referring to Believers

The next thing I want to bring to your attention about these passages is the fact that Jesus is talking about believers here, those who have confessed to make Him Lord and Savior. I bring this up because I hear it said quite often that Jesus is referring to false prophets in these passages, especially about Matthew 7:21–23. This is not so. Jesus is definitely referring to those who have been saved and given His Spirit. As you see here, He clearly says,

> Not everyone who says to me, "Lord, Lord," shall enter the kingdom of heaven. (Matt. 7:21)

Jesus said it is those who call Him Lord that He is referring to here.

Paul tells us,

> Therefore I make known to you that no one speaking by the Spirit of God calls Jesus accursed, and no one can say that Jesus is Lord except by the Holy Spirit. (1 Cor. 12:2)

It is those who have been given His Spirit that call Jesus Lord, and it is those whom He is referring to. Jesus is saying that not all who have confessed Him to be their Lord and Savior, the very ones whom He gave His Spirit to, are going to enter the kingdom of heaven.

Take note here that in Matthew 7:21 and 1 Corinthians 12:2, the word "Lord" is *Kurios*. It is the same word used in both verses as a direct reference to God or the Messiah. So what we see here in 1 Corinthians 12:2, Paul is telling us that we can only speak of Jesus as our Lord (*Kurios*) by the Holy Spirit. That means we have to be commissioned or endued by the Holy Spirit in order to speak of or confess Jesus as our Lord (*Kurios*). His Holy Spirit draws us to Jesus in order to call Him Lord, but Jesus said not everyone who calls Him *Kurios* shall enter the kingdom of heaven but those who do the will of the Father. In other words, we have to be born again with the Word and Spirit, adopted as a child of God and anointed with the Holy Spirit, in order to truly call Jesus our *Kurios*; and by this we will follow Him and do the will of the Father, granting us our place in heaven.

Before you start to say that Jesus is referring to those who falsely call Him Lord, take note that it's quite interesting the three very things Jesus makes reference to in Matthew 7:22: prophesying, casting out demons, and doing many wonders in His name are the same three gifts of the Holy Spirit mentioned in 1 Corinthians 12:10:

> To another the working of miracles, to another prophecy, to another discerning of spirits.

Doing many wonders and working miracles are the same. Prophecy is prophecy, and one must be able to discern spirits in order to cast them out. These are all gifts of the Holy Spirit that are given to those who believe in Christ and are reborn and anointed with the power of the Holy Spirit.

Just so you know, I'm not trying to wrongfully compare these two scriptures together—I'm going to break them down for you. This way you know that the Christ Jesus is referring to those who are reborn and have been given the Holy Spirit. And not all these are going to enter the kingdom of heaven, but those who do the will of the Father. This is very important to know, and you rarely hear of it preached in the church today, if at all.

Now to give you the best definition of what Jesus is saying in Matthew 7:22, and what Paul is telling us in 1 Corinthians 12:10, I will use the King James translation and add in the Greek translation of each key word to show the comparison.

> Many will say to Me in that day, "Lord [*Kurios*], Lord [*Kurios*]," have we not prophesied [*propheteuo*, v] in thy name? And in thy name have cast out devils? And in thy name done many wonderful works [*dunamis*]? (Matt. 7:22 KJV)

And then,

> To another the working of miracles [*dunamis*]; to another prophecy [*propheteia*, n]; to another discerning of spirits; to another divers kinds of tongues; to another the interpretation of tongues. (1 Cor. 12:10 KJV)

As you may now see and understand, Jesus makes reference not only to those who call Him Lord, but also to the gifts that are given by the Holy Spirit. Also take note the Jesus mentions that these gifts were performed in His name, as was said by Jesus,

> Most assuredly, I say to you, he who believes in Me, the works that I do he will do also; and greater works than these he will do, because I go to My Father. And whatever you ask in My name, that I will do, that the Father may be glorified in the Son. (John 14:12–13)

So you see here that these are gifts given by the Holy Spirit and performed by the believer in Christ's name.

One may ask, "Why then would a person who isn't a true believer and is only professing their belief be allowed to perform these gifts of the Holy Spirit?" Remember, it isn't actually the person who performs the gifts or miracles; it's the Holy Spirit. And the person may not actually possess the Holy Spirit at that time; the Holy Spirit may be just working with the person to bring glory to God.

So what we have here is Jesus telling us that not everyone who calls Him Lord, not everyone who does miracles in His name, not everyone who performs any of the wondrous gifts of the Holy Spirit, is going to enter the kingdom of heaven, but only those who do the will of the Father. And what is the will of the Father? The will of the Father is to know God and obey the gospel of the Lord Jesus the Christ. The key words here are "to know" and "obey." I say this is the will of the Father because these are what we must do in order to escape the vengeance of God, these are what we must do in order to become born again, and these are what we must do in order to follow the Christ Jesus, our Lord and Savior. This is what it means to have a relationship with God and follow the Lord Jesus so that we may enter the kingdom of heaven.

Look how Jesus finishes up this statement,

> And then I will declare to them, "I never knew you; depart from Me, you who practice lawlessness!" (Matt. 7:23)

IF WE ARE SAVED, ARE WE PROMISED HEAVEN?

Jesus said, "He will declare to them." The word "declare" here is *homologeo*, the very same word we discussed earlier for "confess." And if you remember, it can be defined as "to promise." Jesus said, "I will declare [*homologeo*] to them, I never knew [*ginosko*] you; depart from Me, you who practice lawlessness!" Jesus is making a declaration or a promise to those who practice lawlessness. What is lawlessness? Is it not disobedience? And if you take notice in this last scripture, Matthew 7:23, the direct relevance to the very things we must do to have everlasting life: confess and know Christ Jesus as Lord and Savior.

Being Cast Out

Let me sum this up for you. Jesus said, "Not everyone who calls Him Lord will enter the kingdom of heaven. And on that day, He will declare to them that He never knew them and to depart from Him, those who practice lawlessness." This brings me to the point about being separated from the presence of God, the very point I mentioned at the beginning of the second chapter, which I said I would come back to:

> These shall be punished with everlasting destruction from the presence of the Lord and from the glory of His power. (2 Cor. 1:9)

Think about the agony and torment one would have to endure, to have experienced the power of the Holy Spirit and be cast from the presence of the Lord Jesus the Christ, and if cast from the presence of the Lord Jesus, then God as well.

Now shortly after Jesus makes this declaration at the end of His sermon on the mountain, the centurion meets Him as He enters Capernaum. This is the centurion who had the paralyzed and dreadfully tormented servant at home and felt that he was unworthy that the Lord should come to his home. So he asked the Lord Jesus to just say the word and the servant would be healed. And when Jesus had heard this, He marveled at such great faith. Jesus said,

> Assuredly, I say to you, I have not found such great faith, not even in Israel! (Matt. 8:10)

We hear of this story taught often in the church, especially on the topic of faith. I mention this story here about the centurion because in church, we don't hear about what Jesus says about the importance of having such faith, right after talking to the centurion. Jesus follows it up with

> And I say to you that many will come from the east and the west, and sit down with Abraham, Isaac, and Jacob in the kingdom of heaven. But the sons of the kingdom will be cast out into outer darkness. There will be weeping and gnashing of teeth. (Matt. 8:11–12)

Jesus just said the sons of the kingdom would be cast out into outer darkness, and there will be weeping and gnashing of teeth. What Jesus is telling us is that some believers' faith is going to be found unapproved. That means they're not truly believers in their hearts, and they are going to be cast out.

Jesus had just finished telling the multitude that not everyone who calls Him Lord would enter the kingdom of heaven, and now He talks about the sons of the kingdom being cast out into outer darkness. Do you think the Lord is referring to the Israelites (Jews), or maybe the Pharisees and the teachers of the law, or unbelievers? He specifically said the sons of the kingdom! Let me tell you, in the monarchy sense of a kingdom, Israel wasn't a kingdom at that time, because they were under the rule of Caesar, the king of Rome.

To fully explain this, so that there isn't any confusion or misinterpretation of what Christ is saying, let's define the meaning of "kingdom." Since the majority of us are worldly, I will use the worldly definition found on Dictionary.com. "Kingdom" (king-duhm) means

1. A state or government having a king or queen as its head.
2. Anything conceived as constituting a realm or sphere of independent action or control: the kingdom of thought.
3. A realm or province of nature, especially one of the three broad divisions of natural objects: the animal, vegetable, and mineral kingdoms.
4. Biology. a taxonomic category of the highest rank, grouping together all forms of life having certain fundamental characteristics in common: in the five-kingdom classification scheme adopted by many biologists, separate kingdoms are assigned to animals (*Animalia*), plants (*Plantae*), fungi (*Fungi*), protozoa and eucaryotic algae (*Protista*), and bacteria and blue-green algae (*Monera*).
5. The spiritual sovereignty of God or Christ.
6. The domain over which the spiritual sovereignty of God or Christ extends, whether in heaven or on earth. (Dictionary.com)

According to this definition, there are only two ways the meaning of "kingdom" can possibly apply to what Christ said. One is the domain over which the spiritual sovereignty of God or Christ extends here on earth. Or we can look at it worldly, a state or government having a king or queen. Now keep in mind what the chief priests said concerning the Jews,

We have no king but Caesar! (John 19:15)

Now that would make the Jews under the rule of the Romans and therefore not a kingdom. The only kingdom Jesus was concerned about was His kingdom, the sovereign spiritual kingdom of God.

Now let's define the word "kingdom" in Greek as it was written originally. The word for "kingdom" is *basileia* (bas-il-i'-ah), meaning

1. Royal power, kingship, dominion, rule
   a) Not to be confused with an actual kingdom but rather the right or authority to rule over a kingdom
   b) Of the royal power of Jesus as the triumphant Messiah
   c) Of the royal power and dignity conferred on Christians in the Messiah's kingdom
2. A kingdom, the territory subject to the rule of a king
3. Used in the N.T. to refer to the reign of the Messiah

Here again, we see the same two meanings that can apply to what Jesus is referring to by the sons of the kingdom. Notice where it says, "Used in the N.T. to refer to the reign of the Messiah," meaning those under the reign of Christ, those who call Jesus Lord. The sons of the kingdom are believers, the followers of Christ Jesus.

Look what Jesus said to His disciples when they asked Him to explain the parable of the tares of the field. He answered and said to them,

> He who sows the good seed is the Son of Man [Jesus]. The field is the world, the good seeds are the sons of the kingdom, but the tares are the sons of the wicked one. (Matt. 13:37–38)

Jesus explains to us here that the sons of the kingdom are those who follow Him, and the sons of the wicked one are those who don't.

IF WE ARE SAVED, ARE WE PROMISED HEAVEN?

And when we follow Jesus, when we make Him our Lord and Savior, we then become adopted as sons of the kingdom, the kingdom of God. I say this again: the sons of the kingdom are the believers in Christ, the ones who have His Spirit and are under His rule, those who call Him Lord and He is their King.

And take note what Jesus says about the tares:

> The Son of Man will send out His angels, and they will gather out of His kingdom all things that offend, and those who practice lawlessness, and will cast them into the furnace of fire. There will be weeping and gnashing of teeth. (Matt. 13:41–42)

Jesus tells us the tares, the sons of the wicked one, will be cast into the furnace of fire or, in other words, the lake of fire. Jesus didn't say outer darkness; He specifically said the furnace of fire. There is a distinct difference between the two, especially since Jesus follows up both sayings with "There will be weeping and gnashing of teeth." Remember, Jesus doesn't mince words; there was a significant meaning to everything He said.

Three times Jesus makes reference to being cast out into outer darkness, all three times He was speaking about the kingdom of heaven, and all three times He is referring to believers. Once was when He was with the centurion and His disciples, stating the importance of faith to enter the kingdom of heaven. The other two were in parables about the kingdom of heaven. And it's quite interesting to note that in both of these parables when He makes this quote, both parables are about finding one approved to enter the kingdom of heaven.

The first parable is in Matthew 22, when Jesus compares the kingdom of heaven to be like a wedding.

> The kingdom of heaven is like a certain king who arranged a marriage for his son, and sent out his servants to call those who were invited to

> the wedding; and they were not willing to come. (Matt. 22:2–3)

The King is God arranging a marriage for His Son, the Christ Jesus; and those who were invited were His people, the Jews. Verses 4–7 are a direct reference to the past, before Christ; and verses 8–10 are in reference to the future after Christ, the new covenant. Jesus tells of the way it was in the old covenant, when only the Jews were invited, and of the way it will be under the new covenant, when all will be invited.

> But when the king came in to see the guests, he saw a man there who did not have on a wedding garment. So he said to him, "Friend, how did you come in here without a wedding garment?" And he was speechless. Then the king said to the servants, "Bind him hand and foot, take him away, and cast him into outer darkness; there will be weeping and gnashing of teeth." For many are called, but few are chosen.

So what Jesus is saying here is that many are called to the body of Christ, but few are chosen or found worthy. Some will be found without the proper attire (being clothed or submerged in Christ) and unapproved to enter the kingdom of heaven. These will be cast into outer darkness.

What does Jesus mean by being found without a wedding garment, or what is the proper attire to be chosen? We can find this answer in the book of Revelation, when Jesus speaks of the Laodicean church, which is the last church before the end of times, today's church. Jesus says,

> I counsel you to buy from Me gold refined in the fire, that you may be rich; and white garments, that the shame of your nakedness may not be revealed; and anoint your eyes with eye salve,

that you may see. As many as I love, I rebuke and chasten. Therefore be zealous and repent. (Rev. 3:18–19)

Jesus tells us to buy from Him gold (knowledge) refined in the fire, that we may be rich (in faith), and white garments (purity), that we may be clothed. That we may be clothed for what? Could it be for the day of judgment?

We learned earlier that we must have a pure heart to see God, and now we have Jesus telling us here we are to buy from Him white garments. If we look at the word for "white" in Greek, it is *leukos* (lyoo-kos'), meaning

1. Light, bright, brilliant
    a) Brilliant from whiteness, (dazzling) white
        1) Of the garments of angels, and of those exalted to the splendor of the heavenly state
        2) Shining or white garments worn on festive or state occasions
        3) of white garments as the sign of innocence and purity of the soul
    b) Dead white
        1) Of the whitening color of ripening grain

So we see here that Jesus could be speaking of the innocence and purity of our souls. An innocence and purity that only comes from abiding in Him; we must be clothed in His righteousness. And it is interesting to note that He said, "I counsel you to buy from Me." Jesus said these white garments, or the purity of our souls is going to cost us something. He didn't say they were free. Could this cost be to make a conscious effort to abide in Him and obey the gospel? Jesus did follow up this scripture with "therefore be zealous and repent."

This brings me to the second parable that Jesus mentions being cast into outer darkness. This parable is about the talents, another parable you hear taught about often in church yet cut short of the significant importance of being found worthy. This parable speaks of the importance of being good and faithful in serving the Lord with whatever He has bestowed upon you to bring Him glory, whether it be money, resources, physical talents, or spiritual gifts.

I find it funny that the majority of the time I hear this parable taught about in church, it's used in comparison to how well one manages their finances and almost entirely directed toward money and the importance of tithing. That is a very narrow interpretation of this parable, and I pray the church doesn't have a hidden agenda behind teaching it with this view. Just because we are to give generously of our resources for the service of the gospel and His kingdom doesn't necessarily mean just our money.

Even though Jesus uses money as the example to explain the importance of managing what God gives us for our service to Him, I find it interesting that He uses the talent for this explanation. Now I could go into detail about the definition of "talent" in Greek, but I think that it's unnecessary here; a talent was indeed a form of money. But what I do find interesting is that out of all the different kinds of money, Jesus does use the talent. I find this interesting only because the meaning of talent is very different today and has nothing to do with money. And remember, Jesus used worldly things as an example of and as a direct reference to spiritual things.

When reading this parable, your focus shouldn't be on money or what the Lord has given you; it should be on your service to Him. The focus of this parable should be on being found approved or worthy to enter into the joy of your Lord. Jesus began this sermon with

Take heed that no one deceives you. (Matt. 24:4)

So don't be deceived into thinking this parable is about money, when it's all about being found good and faithful in using the spiritual gifts He has given you to bring Him glory.

IF WE ARE SAVED, ARE WE PROMISED HEAVEN?

I'm going to break this down for you so you can see that this parable isn't about our money, that it's about our spiritual gifts. Jesus starts this parable with

> For the kingdom of heaven is like a man traveling to a far country, who called his own servants and delivered his goods to them. (Matt. 25:14)

Now the word "delivered" in Greek is *paradidomi* (par-ad-id'-o-mee), meaning

1. To give into the hands (of another)
2. To give over into (one's) power or use
   a) To deliver to one something to keep, use, take care of, manage
   b) To deliver up one to custody, to be judged, condemned, punished, scourged, tormented, put to death
   c) To deliver up treacherously
      1) By betrayal to cause one to be taken
      2) To deliver one to be taught, molded
3. To commit, to commend
4. To deliver verbally
   a) Commands, rites
   b) To deliver by narrating, to report
5. To permit allow
   a) When the fruit will allow that is when its ripeness permits
   b) Gives itself up, presents itself

And the word "goods" in Greek is *huparchonta* (hoop-ar'-khon-tah), meaning

1. Possessions, goods, wealth, property

So what we have here is Jesus explaining that the kingdom of heaven is like the Lord calling His own servants, those who follow Him and giving them His possessions or property, to keep, use, take care of, and manage. Now what is the one possession that Jesus gives us when we confess Him to be our Lord? That's right, He gives us a new spirit; He gives us the Holy Spirit of God. We are adopted in as children of God and given His Spirit with power as a Son of God.

And when you're given the Holy Spirit, He empowers you with certain spiritual gifts or talents, to be used and managed for the edification of the body of Christ, which in turn brings glory to God the Father.

> There are diversities of gifts, but the same Spirit. There are differences of ministries, but the same Lord. And there are diversities of activities, but it is the same God who works all in all. But the manifestation of the Spirit is given to each one for the profit of all: for to one is given the word of wisdom through the Spirit, to another the word of knowledge through the same Spirit, to another faith by the same Spirit, to another gifts of healings by the same Spirit, to another the working of miracles, to another prophecy, to another discerning of spirits, to another different kinds of tongues, to another the interpretation of tongues. But one and the same Spirit works all these things, distributing to each one individually as He wills. (1 Cor. 12:4–11)

So we see here that the Spirit distributes these gifts to each one individually as He sees fit. And in the parable, we have Jesus saying,

> And to one he gave five talents, to another two, and to another one, to each according to his own ability. (Matt. 25:15)

When we put these two scriptures together, we begin to understand that when we are called by the Lord and given His Spirit, we are given certain talents or spiritual gifts that are distributed to each of us according to our ability to manage and use.

And as we continue to read through the parable, we see that the first two servants that Jesus uses as an example for us to follow use the talents given to them to gain more or, in other words, to multiply or grow in the body of Christ.

> Then he who had received the five talents went and traded with them, and made another five talents. And likewise he who had received two gained two more also. (Matt. 25:16–17)

What He is telling us is that when we use or apply the talents that He gives us properly, we increase and grow. And when others see us increasing and growing, they are drawn in, desiring the same thing we have so they too may increase and grow, which in turn builds the body of Christ. When we do this, the Lord will say to us,

> Well done good and faithful servant; you were faithful over a few things, I will make you ruler over many things. Enter into the joy of your Lord. (Matt. 25:21, 23)

> Then he who had received the one talent came and said, "Lord, I knew you to be a hard man, reaping where you have not sown, and gathering where you have not scattered seed." (Matt. 25:24)

Now we see that we, as His servants, are to use these talents to reap and sow for the kingdom of God; we are to use our spiritual gifts to gather more to grow and increase the body of Christ. Jesus isn't talking about money; He is talking about using the possession, the Holy Spirit that He has given you, and the Spirit's gifts to increase and grow the body of Christ and His kingdom. Jesus commissioned us as His servants to

> go therefore and make disciples of all nations, baptizing them in the name of the Father and the Son and of the Holy Spirit. (Matt. 28:19)

And if you don't use the talent to increase and grow, if you hide what the Lord has given you and never apply it, He is not going to be very pleased with you on that last day. Look what He says about the servant that was given one talent when he didn't use it to grow. The servant finished telling Him,

> "And I was afraid, and went and hid your talent in the ground. Look, there you have what is yours." But his lord answered and said to him, "You wicked and lazy servant, you knew that I reap where I have not sown, and gather where I have not scattered seed. So you ought to have deposited my money with the bankers, and at my coming I would have received back my own with interest." (Matt. 25:25–27)

What He is saying here is even if you don't use the talent to reap and sow and gather, at least apply it to the body of Christ to gain interest or help support and edify. You have to apply what the Lord gives you in one way or another for the furtherance of His kingdom. You can't just sit idly by, doing nothing, hiding what He has given you waiting for His return, and think everything is going to be all right.

Look what Jesus says about those who do nothing:

> For to everyone who has, more will be given, and he will have abundance; but from him who does not have, even what he has will be taken away. (Matt. 25:29)

IF WE ARE SAVED, ARE WE PROMISED HEAVEN?

This is where most sermons or teachings on this parable end; they leave out the most significant part that describes the importance of using your spiritual talents properly. Not only that, but they give a total misinterpretation of this scripture as well. That's because all the English translations leave out a very important word that is in the original Greek translation. And when this scripture is properly translated from the Greek, it will bring to light the following scripture:

> And cast the unprofitable servant into the outer darkness. There will be weeping and gnashing of teeth. (Matt. 25:30)

Let's break verse 29 down so you will have a true understanding of what the Lord is saying. I will attempt to keep this as simple as I possibly can. In the King James Version, verse 29 goes like this:

> <u>For</u> unto every <u>one</u> that <u>hath</u> shall be <u>given</u>, <u>and</u> he shall have <u>abundance</u>: <u>but</u> <u>from</u> <u>him</u> that <u>hath</u> <u>not</u> shall be taken <u>away</u> * <u>even</u> that <u>which</u> he <u>hath</u>. (Matt. 25:29 KJV)

All the underlined words are from the Greek transcript, the asterisk (*) denotes the missing word, and the rest are words filled in by translators. Now if I wrote all this out in Greek, it would look like this:

> Gar pas echo didomi, kai perisseuo: de apo autos echo me airo apo kai hos echo.

I have already given you definitions to some of these words in earlier chapters, so I don't have to do it again. And if you notice, we see here the same word *kai* that was used by Jesus when He was speaking of being baptized by water and Spirit (*kai*), but here we see it used in both ways, for "even" and for "and." We also see the word *didomi* again, which means to give, grant, or commission.

Now *gar* (gär) means for.
And *pas* (päs) means

1. Individually
   a) each, every, any, all, the whole, everyone, all things, everything
2. Collectively
   a) Some of all types

Now the word *echo* (e'-khō) means

1. To have, i.e. to hold
   a) To have (hold) in the hand, in the sense of wearing, to have (hold) possession of the mind (refers to alarm, agitating emotions, etc.), to hold fast keep, to have or comprise or involve, to regard or consider or hold as
2. To have i.e. own, possess
   a) External things such as pertain to property or riches or furniture or utensils or goods or food etc.
   b) Used of those joined to any one by the bonds of natural blood or marriage or friendship or duty or law etc., of attendance or companionship
3. To hold one's self or find one's self so and so, to be in such or such a condition
4. To hold one's self to a thing, to lay hold of a thing, to adhere or cling to
   a) To be closely joined to a person or a thing

Let me give you one more definition, and I will put this first part together for you. That word is *perisseuo* (pe-rēs-syü'-ō), meaning

IF WE ARE SAVED, ARE WE PROMISED HEAVEN?

1. To exceed a fixed number of measure, to be left over and above a certain number or measure
   a) To be over, to remain
   b) To exist or be at hand in abundance
      1) To be great (abundant)
      2) A thing which comes in abundance, or overflows unto one, something falls to the lot of one in large measure
      3) To redound unto, turn out abundantly for, a thing
   c) To abound, overflow
      1) To be abundantly furnished with, to have in abundance, abound in (a thing), to be in affluence
      2) To be pre-eminent, to excel
      3) To excel more than, exceed
2. To make to abound
   a) To furnish one richly so that he has abundance
   b) To make abundant or excellent

So the first half of this scripture is telling us that everyone or all who lay ahold of, possess, and are closely joined to Christ shall be given, commissioned, or granted to be made abundant or excellent. Those who are closely joined to Christ will be made righteous!

Which brings us to the second half of this scripture, the part that ties verse 29 to verse 30. The key word in this half, which also just so happens to be the missing word in the English translations, is *apo* (ä-po'), meaning

1. Of separation
   a) Of local separation, after verbs of motion from a place i.e. of departing, of fleeing,
   b) Of separation of a part from the whole

        1) Where of a whole some part is taken
    c) Of any kind of separation of one thing from another by which the union or fellowship of the two is destroyed
    d) Of a state of separation, that is of distance
        1) Physical, of distance of place
        2) Temporal, of distance of time
2. Of origin
    a) Of the place whence anything is, comes, befalls, is taken
    b) Of origin of a cause

And again, let me give you one more definition before I put this half together, and that is *airo* (ī'-rō), meaning

1. To raise up, elevate, lift up
    a) To raise from the ground, take up: stones
    b) To raise upwards, elevate, lift up: the hand
    c) To draw up: a fish
2. To take upon one's self and carry what has been raised up, to bear
3. To bear away what has been raised, carry off
    a) To move from its place
    b) To take off or away what is attached to anything
    c) To remove
    d) To carry off, carry away with one
    e) To appropriate what is taken
    f) To take away from another what is his or what is committed to him, to take by force
    g) To take and apply to any use

h) To take from among the living, either by a natural death, or by violence
i) Cause to cease

And the second half of this scripture is telling us, "The origin or place taken of him or her, which is joined not (to Christ), will be taken by force or carried off, being separated from that which was once joined." It's the same thing Jesus has been telling us all throughout His gospel that if we don't join ourselves to Him and abide in Him, take His yoke upon us and learn from Him, deny ourselves to follow and serve Him, we have no life in us and what He has given us will be taken away and we will be separated from Him.

As you may begin to understand, this parable isn't about managing our money; it's about using the precious gift of His Holy Spirit to serve Him, and if we don't, we will be considered to be an unprofitable servant and cast out into outer darkness; we will be considered unworthy and separated from His light and glory. Again, this is why Jesus told us not to be deceived; this is why it is so important to spend time learning God's Word. When you make Jesus your Lord and Savior, you're to take what He has given you and use it to serve Him and His kingdom; you're to use it to bring Him glory. If you receive His Spirit and don't apply it to make changes in your life, to the point that people see His light in you and are drawn to Him, that is the same as hiding what He has given you in the ground, and you will be considered an unprofitable servant. This is what Jesus is telling us in this parable. Remember Jesus said,

> He who is not with Me is against Me, and he who does not gather with Me scatters abroad. (Matt. 12:30)

Hot or Cold

You may think that I'm being too literal or overly strict about God's Word and that I'm taking it too far, and that's fine. Many people have told me this many times. I've even been ridiculed and persecuted by friends, family, and other Christians; and I believe the list has only begun. Thank You, Jesus. My own mother told me I was a borderline radical extremist and that I take this too seriously and I need to let up some because people are going to start saying things about me. She said I am so radical and extreme about Jesus and God's Word that she compared me to a terrorist in another country. Thank You, Jesus! I would like to believe she is right, although I know in my heart that I could be more radical and extreme for my Lord, and I'm working on it, because that is exactly what Jesus wants; He wants us to be on fire for Him!

Look what Jesus says about the end-time church, our time; this is the church of today. Now mind you, Jesus is saying this about His church, the body of Christ.

> These things says the Amen, the Faithful and True Witness, the Beginning of the creation of God: "I know your works, that you are neither cold nor hot. I could wish you were cold or hot. So then, because you are lukewarm, and neither cold nor hot, I will vomit you out of My mouth." (Rev. 3:14–16)

You catch that? When you sit idly by doing nothing, you make Him sick. He said He will vomit you out of His mouth! Does that sound like you are going to heaven?

The word here for "vomit" is *emeo* (em-eh'-o), meaning

1. To vomit, vomit forth, throw up

And let me tell you, this is the only time this word is used in the entire Bible. Nowhere else is this word used at all! God and the Lord Jesus are serious about our service to the kingdom of God and our hearts being for Him. This isn't a game, people. If you call Jesus Lord and you're not hot or on fire for Him, that means if you're not serving Him, you are making Him sick. He will say, "Depart from

Me, you lazy and unprofitable servant," and He will cast you out and separate you from Him.

Let me put it this way: every day you parade around calling yourself a Christian, a follower of Christ, and you intentionally live a disobedient life, you have the Accuser going before God saying, "This is your child? You think he or she loves you? Look what he or she is doing now. They say they love You, but they don't show it. They don't care about You, God. They only care about themselves and are just taking advantage of Your grace." Satan is constantly reminding Christ Jesus that every intentional sin and act of disobedience shows the Christians' heart isn't truly for the Lord, that they love themselves more than the One who gave His life for them. Satan is making a mockery of the body of Christ and rubbing it in God's face every day, and we are just sitting idly by letting him do it because we put more faith in the furniture we sit on than we do in our Creator, the God Almighty. Do you think that after living your life, saying how much you love the Lord Jesus and God and never showing it, He is going to say all is well?

On the day of judgment, when you're on your knees before the Lord Jesus, will you be found as a true and faithful servant? Or will your name and the life you lived be found lukewarm, leaving a bitter taste in the Lord's mouth? Will you have taken the conscious effort to know God? Will you have been born again and lived a life worthy of His praise? Will you have taken the free gift given to you and put it to work in your life so that you may be found acceptable to enter into His presence (heaven) for all eternity?

The End

> And behold, I am coming quickly,
> And My reward is with Me, to give to
> every one according to his work.
> I am the Alpha and Omega, the Beginning
> and the End, the First and the Last.
>
> —Revelation 22:12–13

The intention of this book is to encourage the Christian to read their Bible and get to know the Almighty God and Christ Jesus, our Lord and Savior. It is meant to persuade the reader the importance of making a conscious effort to show your faith and belief in Christ Jesus by living in obedience to Him and the Word of God.

Could you imagine what this world would be like if everyone read his or her Bibles on a daily basis and lived in obedience to the Word of God? People would be courteous and loving to one another; they would be helpful and encouraging. People wouldn't lie, cheat, and steal from one another because there wouldn't be any need to do so. The inequality in society would be practically obsolete, and everyone would have jobs with great pay. There wouldn't be people starving or homeless, and poverty would be nonexistent.

Instead, the world we live in today is messed up; it's horrible! People are unloving and mean to each other. They care only of themselves, and even then they are still miserable. With social media, people are bashed and teased now by others from all over the globe; they are trashed and beat down by people who don't even have a clue of who the person is or what they are going through. When did we become so heartless?

My wife read a story to me the other day about an elderly man who was arrested and put in jail for feeding the homeless. Apparently, some lawmakers in one of our great cities have decided that if they pass a law prohibiting people from sharing food with the displaced, then the displaced would then ultimately leave their city. Where is our humanity?

These are only a couple of examples of how terrible society is today. I could go on and on, but there is no need. All you have to do is turn on the local news to see how bad things truly are. You hear people say quite often, "If God is so loving, then why does He allow all these evil and tragic things to happen?" It's very simple really; He loves us so much that He gave us the freedom of choice, to choose for ourselves what we want.

Therefore, as we live our lives, we are faced with many choices throughout it. The choices we make define us as who we are, what kind of life we want to live, and the paths we take to achieve our role in this world. I believe the ultimate choice we have in life is whether we chose to believe in God or deny Him. Everyone in this world will come to a time in their life where they will have to make this choice. There are no exceptions; it's inevitable.

People desperately need a Savior in this world today. God wants people to experience His salvation here and now and save us, but we first must turn our hearts to Him. The problem is, people don't turn their hearts to God because they don't see the true power of God being displayed in the body of Christ, the church. The true miraculous power of God Almighty cannot be seen because of the lack of obedience and compromise being demonstrated by the Christian community and church.

Disobedience shows disbelief, because if you truly believed in God and Christ Jesus and knew there were consequences for every sin you commit, then you wouldn't intentionally sin. Compromise shows lack of faith, because if you truly trust the Lord Jesus and have saving faith in the God Almighty, then you would stand firm in the

Word of God; there wouldn't be any compromise in your integrity or actions to conform to the world or its ways.

Without true faith and true belief in Christ Jesus and the Almighty God, the believer cannot manifest the true miraculous healing power of God's salvation. Our churches compromise their actions and the message they preach in order to conform to the people's desires, instead of having faith in the very One they teach. They are left begging God for healing and revival in their church when they should already be filled with and possess the supernatural healing power of God.

God loves us so much that He sent His Son to live among us, to teach us, and then to die for our sin against Him. God did this so we would have a way to spend all eternity with Him, in His presence, through our faith and belief in Christ Jesus. Christ Jesus did what we couldn't do, and that is make atonement for our sins so that we may dwell once again in the presence of God. Christ Jesus did the work to provide the way, but we must do the work to follow the way He provided.

At the end of the Bible, in the book of Revelations, the Lord Jesus testifies to the churches,

> And behold, I am coming quickly, and My reward is with Me, to give to every one according to his work. I am the Alpha and Omega, the Beginning and the End, the First and the Last. (Rev. 22:12–13)

The word here for "reward" is *misthos* (mēs-tho's), meaning

1. Dues paid for work
    a) Wages, hire
2. Reward: used of the fruit naturally resulting from toils and endeavors-of divine recompense
    a) In both senses, rewards and punishments

> b) Of the rewards which God bestows, or will bestow, upon good deeds and endeavors
> c) Of punishments

I find it interesting that the translators would use the word "reward" when a better translation would have been "payment." The Lord Jesus is going to return, and each of us who call ourselves a believer is going to get our due, whether it be rewards or punishments. My question to you is are you a true believer, and do your actions prove it? Or are you just professing a faith and belief in Christ for a free ride to the promise land?

Jesus tells us that our dues are with Him, according to our work. Is how we live our life and treat others the work He is speaking of? Could it be how we contribute to the body of Christ and our obedience to Him? Jesus said,

> A new commandment I give to you, that you love one another; as I have loved you, that you also love one another. By this all will know that you are My disciples, if you have love for one another. (John 13:34–35)

Paul wrote,

> Therefore be imitators of God as dear children. And walk in love, as Christ also has loved us and given Himself for us, an offering and sacrifice to God for a sweet-smelling aroma. But fornication and all uncleanness or covetousness, let it not even be named among you, as is fitting for saints; neither filthiness, nor foolish talking, nor coarse jesting, which are not fitting, but rather giving of thanks. For this you know, that no fornicator, unclean person, nor covetous man, who is an idolater, has any inheritance in the king-

> dom of Christ and God. Let no one deceive you with empty words, for because of these things the wrath of God comes upon the sons of disobedience. Therefore do not be partakers with them. (Eph. 5:1–7)

The choice is all yours in how you want to live and what you want to believe. You can believe in Christ Jesus and follow His commandments and live. Or you can deny God and follow this world and its ways and die. The choice is all yours!

> He who is unjust, let him be unjust still; he who is filthy, let him be filthy still; he who is righteous, let him be righteous still; he who is holy, let him be holy still. (Rev. 22:11)

This brings me to the following question: if we are saved, are we promised heaven? The answer to that question is if you know God and have submerged yourself in Christ Jesus, opening your heart to Him in love to the point of obedience, allowing His light to be clearly seen through you in your actions and deeds, and being filled with the Holy Spirit and truly born again, then salvation is yours; and you will spend eternity with Him in heaven.

If you proclaim the Christ Jesus to be your Lord and Savior and don't spend time reading the Word of God, learning the gospel, and applying it to your life, then you're the same as a liar and a thief. You are deceived and only think you are saved. You will stand before the judgment seat of Christ Jesus and take the chance of being separated to the left, and He will declare to you,

> Depart from Me, you cursed, into the everlasting fire prepared for the devil and his angels. (Matt. 25:41)

IF WE ARE SAVED, ARE WE PROMISED HEAVEN?

I call you a liar, because the Word says,

> He who says, "I know Him," and does not keep His commandments, is a liar, and the truth is not in him. (1 John 2:4)

> If someone says, "I love God," and hates his brother, he is a liar; for he who does not love his brother whom he has seen, how can he love God whom he has not seen? (1 John 4:20)

> Whoever believes that Jesus is the Christ is born of God, and everyone who loves Him who begot [the Father] also loves him who is begotten of Him. By this we know that we love the children of God, when we love God and keep His commandments. (1 John 5:1–2)

If you call Jesus "Lord" and your actions don't show it, then you are a liar.

Repent today and be saved!

I call you a thief, because if you think you can just enter the kingdom of heaven without striving to enter through the narrow gate and fighting the good fight of faith, then you are the same as a thief and a robber. Jesus said,

> Most assuredly, I say to you, he who does not enter the sheepfold by the door, but climbs up some other way, the same is a thief and a robber. (John 10:1)

If you think you can call Jesus "Lord" and continue to live your life, committing intentional sin thinking it's okay because you are forgiven, doing whatever you please in full disregard of His Word and commands, then you are stealing from God grace and mercy.

Repent today and be saved!

Jesus said,

> Not everyone who says to Me, "Lord, Lord," shall enter the kingdom of heaven, but he who does the will of My Father in heaven. (Matt. 7:21)

The will of the Father is simple: to know (*ginosko*) God, believe (*pisteuo*) in the Son, and obey the gospel. All it takes for you to do is open your heart to Christ Jesus, read and learn the Word of God, and make a conscious effort to apply it to your life.

Repent today, for the kingdom of heaven is at hand!

Well, it's time for me to wrap this book up and leave you to decide for yourself on what you want to believe. I hope and pray that you are inspired by what you have read in this book and take action toward your destiny and begin to have a loving relationship with God and the Christ Jesus. I hope and pray that you take the first step to your salvation and pick up your Bible and begin to read it on a regular basis and devour the scriptures, allowing them to take root in your heart and renew your mind.

Repent, for the kingdom of heaven is at hand.

About the Author

At the age of fifty-four, Brandon Dover currently still resides in his hometown of Las Vegas, Nevada. Unlike the weather, living in Las Vegas has been far from being sunny and bright for Brandon. He started smoking marijuana at the age of fourteen and was addicted to methamphetamines and became a high school dropout by the age of seventeen. At that time, Brandon was working as a full-time carpenter with big dreams of becoming a successful homebuilder. After twenty-five years of living a life ravaged by drug addiction, Brandon has undergone dozens of treatment programs, has gone through two divorces and two prison sentences, had both his children taken from him, is now considered a career criminal, and has become somewhat unemployable to this day. Amid all the pain and turmoil Brandon endured from his drug addiction, God has always had His hand upon Brandon, knocking on his heart.

Today Brandon lives a life full of peace and joy by the grace of God Almighty. God has put a hedge around Brandon, protects him, and blesses everything he lays his hand to do. Brandon has experienced the miraculous healing power of God, from his drug addiction to surviving a series of severe heart attacks that lasted several days. Brandon is living in great health, is now blessed with six children, and has a beautiful Christian wife.

Brandon has written this book out of experiencing the true salvation of Christ Jesus.

Thank You, Jesus!

Printed in the USA
CPSIA information can be obtained
at www.ICGtesting.com
CBHW051740260224
4659CB00033B/274